T0339487

"When the COVID-19 pandemic first hit, the word 'unprecedented' was thrown around a lot—in part, as a way to wrap our heads around all the sudden disruptions to our lives. It was also a convenient and seemingly acceptable way for public health officials, school superintendents, employers, and city, state, and federal government officials to rationalize any missteps in their pandemic response and communication along the way.

And while the COVID-19 pandemic has been, in a way, unprecedented—in that as Americans, most of us haven't been directly impacted to this extent by a public health emergency of this scale before—it's far from the first time an infectious disease has disrupted entire societies. But instead of learning from challenges and successes of the past, the overwhelming sentiment among policymakers was that we had to start from scratch, and guess our way through the pandemic as it killed hundreds or thousands of people each day.

But thanks to the work of public health communication experts like Dr. Amelia Burke-Garcia, this won't be the case when we're staring down the next pandemic or public health emergency. In her book, *Communicating Through a Pandemic: A Chronicle of Experiences, Lessons Learned, and a Vision for the Future,* Burke-Garcia draws on her personal and professional experiences during the COVID-19 pandemic, as well as the messaging from previous pandemics, to create a tool for both understanding and engaging in meaningful and effective public health communication—particularly in emergency situations.

Burke-Garcia's accessible writing style and format meets the reader where they are and includes definitions of words and phrases that, previous to COVID-19, were typically confined to a particular profession, but now have gone mainstream. She also clears up concepts crucial to communication, like 'misinformation' and 'disinformation,' that can be difficult to keep straight, even for seasoned professionals.

Although it would behoove public health officials and others tasked with public-health-related messaging to read the book in its entirety, Burke-Garcia structured it in a way that allows readers to use it as a reference, turning to the chapter they need when they need it, so the information is easy to locate and immediately digestible.

Another standout aspect of Burke-Garcia's work is her inclusive approach to public health and the different types of communication it requires. This ranges from the impact of COVID-19 on our individual and collective mental health to a look at social determinants of health for different racial and ethnic communities, to highlighting the experiences of groups often left out of public discourse, including people experiencing housing insecurity, migrant and farm workers, and essential workers.

Communicating Through a Pandemic is an indispensable resource for those involved with public health decision-making and messaging, and an illuminating read for anyone looking to gain a deeper understanding of pandemic communication in general, or, more specifically, the reasoning behind and effects of the messaging we've received over the past two years."

Elizabeth Yuko, PhD, *bioethicist and* Rolling Stone *contributing editor*

"Dr. Amelia Burke-Garcia's book, *Communicating Through a Pandemic: A Chronicle of Experiences, Lessons Learned, and a Vision for the Future*, is one of the best health communication science books I've read in years. Her writing is vulnerable, at times, humorous, honest, and most importantly, educative. She shows us the intersection of COVID-19, emotional health, disparities, and inequality, and by creating *How Right Now!*, she reveals that there is hope, human kindness, and resilience amid a global pandemic. Dr. Burke-Garcia is a masterful storyteller, as she eloquently describes her COVID-19 experience, the dimensions of emergency response, and expertly guides the reader through creating *How Right Now!*, which embodies the spirit of Ubuntu: 'I am because we are.' Her book is the foundation we need for our village to be, and do, better in the future."

Ashani Johnson-Turbes, PhD, *Vice President & Director of the Center on Equity Research, NORC at the University of Chicago and Vice President, Society for Health Communication*

"Dr. Amelia Burke-Garcia has written an indispensable guide to communicating for better public health—better health, period, of all Americans. Data show that telling and sharing our stories improves health outcomes. There's no better medium than digital and social media for doing this—and Dr. Burke-Garcia gives us a guide."

Morra Aaron-Mele, *Executive Vice President of Social Impact at Geben Communication, Founder of Women Online and The Mission List, Author of the book,* Hiding in the Bathroom: An Introvert's Roadmap to Getting Out There (When You'd Rather Stay Home), *and host of the Anxious Achiever Podcast for LinkedIn Presents*

"With a mix of personal anecdote, compassionate reflection, and expert insight, Dr. Amelia Burke-Garcia demonstrates the crucial role context plays in public health messaging: What we're going through can impact what information we see and how we perceive it … This book should serve as a road map for pandemic communicators—what we've done and what we could do better."

Robyn Correll Carlyle, MPH, *Public Health Consultant*

"*Communicating Through a Pandemic: A Chronicle of Experiences, Lessons Learned, and a Vision for the Future* by Dr. Amelia Burke-Garcia is a must read for communications professionals, not just in the public health field but in every field. As Dr. Burke-Garcia takes us through the history of pandemic communication, leading up to where we are today, it's clear that not only her deep understanding of public health communication, but her big picture, nuanced perspective provides much-needed navigational guidance for where we go next. Thank you Dr. Burke-Garcia for providing this communication roadmap, filled with context and insight, for a crisis that certainly needs one."

Cooper Munroe, *Founder and CEO, The Motherhood*

"As the pandemic pressed in on all of us, isolating us from the lives and the people that we had come to know and love, it began to take a toll in ways many of us could never have imagined. Not only were we wrestling to make sense of a strange new disease, the illnesses it was causing, and the deaths it left in its wake, but we also began witnessing mental health concerns with little understanding of what was happening.

In her book, Dr. Amelia Burke-Garcia walks us through that process and how it helped birth a mental health, coping, and resilience campaign called *How Right Now* (or *Que Hacer Ahora*, in Spanish). She shares insights and information on what she learned through her work with the Centers for Disease Control and Prevention and how we can learn from this pandemic so that when the next one rolls around, we can do better at not only disseminating information but helping people to cope.

Burke-Garcia's personal and relatable style throughout the book provides an engaging and authentic look at her own experience as well as ties in what was happening in the world around us. She begins by building a foundation rich with science and data that not only helps the reader make sense of where the book is going but lends to its credibility. She also explores the media's role, the impact of social media, and the mixed messages people have received throughout—all of which can have an impact on a person's understanding of and response to the pandemic.

This book makes a wonderful resource for those who work in public health or even mental health, but it also is a useful read for anyone who has lived through COVID-19. Not only are the anecdotes relatable, but reading the experiences of others resonates with readers and lets them know they are not alone in their experiences—there are other people out there who are going through the same thing. This book also provides an insightful and thought-provoking history of what our country—as well as the world—experienced.

As Burke-Garcia reminds us, we can learn from this pandemic and get better at communicating true information during public health crises. We can learn how to utilize social media to support our messages rather than allow it to work against us and she willingly shares her ideas and experiences in an insightful and thought-provoking way. And, even though our world may be different than it was pre-pandemic, Burke-Garcia's book reminds us that there is still hope."

Sherri Gordon *is an author and contributing writer for VeryWellFamily. She is also a bullying prevention and healthy relationship advocate and writes regularly about parenting, mental health, and technology.*

Communicating Through a Pandemic

Outbreaks, epidemics, and pandemics are nothing new and over the course of the last several decades, we have been through numerous ones—Zika, Ebola, H1N1. The COVID-19 pandemic, however, has challenged us like never before. During this time, we have struggled to work remotely, to balance work and children's school schedules, and to manage finances in the face of lost or furloughed jobs. We have worried about our loved ones getting sick and being able to support themselves, and we have faced the loneliness that comes with social distancing.

It has affected us individually and globally—but we have not all experienced this pandemic in exactly the same way. Some communities have been hit harder in terms of sickness and death rates from COVID-19. Many have felt the economic pressures of the pandemic more acutely. Still others have struggled disproportionately with the mental health impacts. Context has mattered in this pandemic.

There is one common thread that runs through all we have experienced though: The role that communication has played in managing this pandemic. Whether we are talking about communication about the virus and mitigation strategies, communication between friends and family, the urgent crisis that is mis- and dis-information, our complex and diffuse media environment, or new workplace communication strategies, communication has been front and center in this pandemic.

The role of communication has been integral to the success *and* failure of our ability to respond and adapt to and begin to recover from this pandemic—as individuals, as communities, and as countries. As a result, issues such as preparedness, misinformation, literacy and comprehension of virus and vaccine science, health equity and mental health have all gained increased awareness during this time.

This book unpacks the many and varied roles that communication has played over the course of this pandemic in order to help public health professionals, marketers and health communicators, and policymakers alike understand what we have been through, what has worked well, and what we have struggled with—personally in our lives and collectively in our communities—in order to be able to address future pandemics more successfully. It can help us learn from this experience and get better at communicating through pandemics in the future.

Communicating Through a Pandemic

A Chronicle of Experiences, Lessons Learned, and a Vision for the Future

Amelia Burke-Garcia, PhD

Routledge
Taylor & Francis Group

A PRODUCTIVITY PRESS BOOK

First published 2023
by Routledge
605 Third Avenue, New York, NY 10158

and by Routledge
4 Park Square, Milton Park, Abingdon, Oxon, OX14 4RN

Routledge is an imprint of the Taylor & Francis Group, an informa business

ISBN: 978-1-032-21254-8 (hbk)
ISBN: 978-1-032-21253-1 (pbk)
ISBN: 978-1-003-26752-2 (ebk)

DOI: 10.4324/9781003267522

Typeset in AGaramond
by MPS Limited, Dehradun

To Betsy, Jorge, Allison, Kathy, Cynthia, Pierce, Turquoise, and Craig.

And to all the public health professionals who have worked so hard and given up so much over the course of this pandemic.

This book is for you.

Thank you.

In loving memory of Bear

January 28, 2010–October 21, 2021

Contents

Foreword

The COVID-19 Pandemic has touched us all in one way or another, some of us more acutely, such as those who have experienced the loss of loved ones, isolation, depression, fear, or anxiety. For others it has led to disruptions to our livelihoods, persistent stressors, changes in lifestyles, uptake of technology and devices, or wide range of emotional challenges. Dr. Burke-Garcia captures these types of experiences in this book as she shares her story during the COVID-19 pandemic and her significant leadership role in the Centers for Disease Control and Prevention (CDC) campaign, *How Right Now/Qué Hacer Ahora*.

Storytelling is a powerful method of sharing personal and professional experiences unique to our lives, our work, our community, our society, and our globe. This phenomenological viewpoint shares real-life experiences to give a deeper sense of understanding about the impact pandemics have on mental health. What we know is that COVID-19 is not only an infectious disease, but a shared collective experience.

Dr. Burke-Garcia takes us through her personal journey during COVID-19 and walks us through initiation, development, and roll out of the *How Right Now/Qué Hacer Ahora* campaign. She gives us an important view of the public health challenges facing America today and the complicated pandemic communication environment. She is introspective, factual, hopeful, and grateful to share her story. Every word, sentence, paragraph, and chapter are devoted to informing and educating us about this pandemic and efforts to mitigate its spread. The story of COVID-19 is the ubiquitous story of those impacted and infected, those hospitalized, in recovery, uninfected by the virus, tragedies and traumas, the public health response to the pandemic, the accumulative losses and extended grieving, the mixed social messaging and informational challenges spread across the health communication environment. She carefully describes the persistent and evasive characteristics of the infectious disease and its effect on our mental health.

The campaign promulgated by CDC and supported by the CDC Foundation was researched and operationalized by NORC at the University of Chicago. By any measure it was an early and quick response to inform the public with facts, describing risks, and encouraging self-efficacy and norms about mitigating the spread of the infectious disease. Much was learned by the team who were informed by research participants' stories of either being impacted or infected by COVID-19. The *How Right Now/Qué Hacer Ahora* team, made up of experts from across the country, worked together at an accelerated pace and in a virtual environment at the onset of COVID-19 in the spring 2020 through its formal launch in August 2020 as the number of COVID-19 cases was proliferating.

As you read about the campaign's informative research methods that helped craft messages in English and Spanish, it focuses on the mental health impact of COVID-19 on diverse groups who were, have been, and will continue to be adversely impacted by an infectious disease that has yet to meet its own demise. Genuine and culturally informed outreach and engagement was deployed by design and not as an afterthought. The longstanding advocate mantra "nothing about us without us" tapped into the cultural brokers from the diverse communities sought for the formative research.

Communities of color, such as Latinos, were disproportionately infected, hospitalized, dying, unemployed, unsheltered, hungry, and left in a maze of misinformation or uncertainty. The initial, arduous, and incremental roll out of personal protective equipment (PPE) and the challenge to expedite the development of the COVID-19 vaccines, combined by conflicting messages at the local, state, and federal levels all played a role in who people felt they could trust and what they believed was the right thing to do. Meanwhile, essential workers were and continue to be exposed at work and in educational settings, which has impacted America's workforce in all sectors. The campaign's important focus on the emotional well-being addressed the increasing and persistent stressors on our personal and collective mental health. Research participants openly expressed their heartfelt emotions in genuine and raw form. America as a nation is also experiencing collective emotional strain and pain caused by this pandemic. You will be touched by the personal testimonial vignettes found in this book. They remind us of our shared vulnerability, humanity, and resilience.

This book is not only a must-read but also a tool for all of us to use. As a retrospect of the last two years of the pandemic in the U.S., it captures the onset, twists and turns, valleys, and pinnacles of the pandemic. But most of all, it informs us of what we can do to help ourselves, our families, our neighborhoods, our friends, our community, our nation, and our fellow human beings. In part, I feel the public health imperative to encourage my colleagues, Latino cohorts, health care providers, community members, parents, educators, policy leaders, public health, and mental health leaders to learn and participate in the *How Right Now/Qué Hacer Ahora* campaign. It helps us make sense of the factors that have consumed our lives the last two years and learn what more can be done together—How and Right Now!

Let's not forget those individuals continuing to fight this infection for the benefit of everyone and not just some. This story will inspire you to continue to combat our common enemy: COVID-19. Let's work together to extinguish this pandemic. Let's find new messages tailored to individuals and communities to build on the successes of this campaign and others to mitigate the spread of COVID-19. Let's continue to reach out to the most vulnerable of our society so that we can bring more light to a dark chapter in our nation's public health and mental health story. They are not hard to reach, they live in our neighborhoods, communities, and among us.

Join me in thanking Dr. Burke-Garcia for sharing her story—a story of hope. The next phase of the campaign must now reach into the deepest crevices of our systemic and social structures so that we can build our collective resiliency to protect, promote, and preserve our well-being as a nation, now and in the future.

Fredrick Sandoval, MPA
Executive Director
National Latino Behavioral Health Association

About the Author

Dr. Amelia Burke-Garcia is an award-winning health communication professional, author, and keynote speaker. With a background in health communication program planning, implementation, and evaluation, her career spans several decades. She currently acts as the Program Area Director, Digital Strategy and Outreach, at NORC at the University of Chicago, where she designs and implements strategies that leverage the power of digital media to influence behavior. She currently oversees the award-winning *How Right Now/Que Hacer Ahora* campaign, which aims to increase people's ability to cope and be resilient amidst the COVID-19 pandemic. She also currently leads several studies focused on exploring social media influencers and vaccine hesitancy. Over the course of her career, Dr. Burke-Garcia has spearheaded some of the most innovative communication programs and studies on a variety of health topics, including designing a targeted social media intervention with mommy bloggers to help social media users lower their risk for breast cancer, and leveraging MeetUp groups and the Waze mobile application to move people to action around flu vaccination and HIV testing, respectively. She is widely published and the author of the book, *Influencing Health: A Comprehensive Guide to Working with Social Media Influencers*, which came out in 2019. She has been highlighted by the U.S. Surgeon General, Dr. Vivek Murthy, for her work in honor of Women's History Month and has been named to VeryWellHealth.com's list of 10 Modern Female Innovators Shaking Up Health Care. She holds a PhD in Communication from George Mason University, a Master's degree in Communication, Culture, and Technology from Georgetown University, and a joint honours Bachelor's degree in International Development Studies and Humanistic Studies from McGill University.

Notes to the Reader

Before we begin, I want to share a couple of things with you related to the scope of this book.

First, this book was written over the course of the pandemic and as such, it has been written in a tense that reflects that time period. Therefore, despite President Biden declaring the COVID-19 pandemic over on September 18, 2022, this book is written from the perspective of still being in the pandemic.

As well, I want to note that I mostly use the term, "COVID," throughout this book (rather than specifically, "COVID-19"). This is intentional as I refer to COVID both as a virus and pandemic as well as a time period and set of experiences we have all gone through.

I also want to take a moment to acknowledge a few colleagues who contributed in various ways to this book. First, Bryan Gustafson helped me with reviewing articles for Chapter 5. Second, two of my *How Right Now* team members, Ms. Lily McCutchan (who previously worked with me at NORC at the University of Chicago) and Ms. Carol Schadelbauer (who works for Burness Communications) helped me in thinking through the qualities of our team for Chapter 9. And Erin Cutroneo helped with the design of Figure 5.1.

Finally, I want to note that throughout this book, we will cover numerous difficult topics including discussions of death, depression, suicide and suicidal ideation, trauma, racism, and hate crimes. I want you to be prepared for the discussions of these topics in the pages that follow and to know that if you are not comfortable with them, it is ok to skip sections and read this book so that it is fitting and useful for you.

And if you are experiencing a crisis right now, you can find help at the resources below:

- National Suicide Prevention Lifeline: 988
- National Domestic Violence Hotline: 1-800-799-7233

- National Sexual Assault Hotline: 1-800-656-HOPE (4673) (para español presiona el 2)
- National Child Abuse Hotline: 1-800-4AChild (1-800-422-4453)
- The Trevor Project's Lifeline: 1-866-488-7386
- Veteran's Crisis Line: 1-800-273-TALK (8255)

Thank you.

Chapter 1

Introduction—A.K.A. My Pandemic Story

The secret of change is to focus all of your energy,
not on fighting the old, but on building the new.

—*Socrates*

I started writing this book as a way to process what I have been through over the course of this pandemic. As a way to understand the magnitude of what we all have been through during this time. However, it has been hard to figure out how to really articulate what the past several years have been like.

On the one hand, I have been in the same boat as many of you. Stuck at home, socially isolated from many of the people and things I love, worried about getting sick or someone I love getting sick, worried about new variants, watching many people (including some I have known) die from COVID, feeling frustrated by people refusing the vaccine in the face of so much death, feeling hopeless at times when it felt like this situation would drag on forever; all-the-while trying to figure out how to keep living my life during a pandemic.

You know. All those things that we all have gone through. Those feelings and experiences that have been universal.

On the other hand, my experiences have also not been like the experiences of others. Generally, I have managed through it all OK. I have been lucky not to have had to struggle *that much* during this pandemic. I am fortunate to have a job that I can do from my home. I am fortunate enough to have a home and can

DOI: 10.4324/9781003267522-1

still afford that home. And I am fortunate enough to have enough space in my home to transition to remote work and social distancing comfortably.

I am an educated white woman with a PhD. I work in private industry. I can do my job on my computer from anywhere. I have health insurance. Financially, I have not struggled as so many others have.

I am aware of this privilege.

I also do not have children, which has made my life working remotely with my husband MUCH easier. The balancing act that so many people have had to figure out in COVID because of telework and teleschool, among other things, has not been something I have had to deal with.

For all of these reasons, COVID has not impacted me the way it has impacted so many other people.

So while some of my experiences in COVID may have been universal, many of them have not been. I have been one of the fortunate ones.

We have all been through the same pandemic, and yet, we have not experienced it in quite the same way. COVID has raised to the forefront of our consciousnesses issues of inequality. Of disparities. Of racism (both individual and systemic). Issues that have long existed. Issues that many of us are just seeing now more clearly because of what has been brought to light in the pandemic.

Yet, despite the many privileges that I have, the pandemic has still been hard for me. As it has been for so many.

It is undeniable: This period of time. Has. Been. Tough.

I started writing this book to share what it has been like. For me. For others. I wanted to understand what it has all meant. I wanted to talk about the various dimensions of what we have all gone through—together and individually. And I wanted to do this by telling a story—one that draws on data as well as people's personal experiences. One that is told through my personal point of view.

This is that story. My pandemic story.

The Struggle Has Been Real

Over the course of this book, we are going to talk about a lot of aspects of COVID that have impacted our lives. Difficult ones. Silver linings. Things such as:

Sickness.

Death.

Quarantining.

Lockdowns.

Economic turmoil.

Masking.

Fighting.

Confusing and conflicting messaging.

Vaccines.

Variants.

Community.

Coping.

Resilience.

Misinformation (or information that is false but believed to be true by the person spreading it).[1]

Disinformation (or information that is false and known to be false by the person spreading it).[2]

Information overload.

Social connectedness.

Before we get into those topics, though, I want to talk a little bit about one topic in particular.

That is: Fatigue.

Because, man, I am tired.

And that is despite most of my activities having been taken away during COVID! Until recently, I had not gone to an in-studio yoga class. Until recently, I had not traveled on a plane. Until recently, I had not eaten out at a restaurant with other people.

Yet, I feel exhausted. I think many of you know what I am talking about.

In fact, there has been a lot written about the topic of fatigue over the course of the pandemic. Lisa Olivera, a marriage and family therapist based in Berkeley, California, talks about how, in COVID, we have had to deal with much more stress over a much longer period of time than we normally do.[3] This kind of stress activates our "fight or flight" response, which, in normal circumstances, is a typical and healthy response; but when activated for such a long period of time, and by something that we cannot control, can substantially impact our mental and physical well-being. And this "chronic stress" can cause "fatigue, problems concentrating, irritability, and changes in sleep and appetite," according to Inger Burnett-Zeigler, an associate professor of psychiatry at Northwestern University.[4]

In short, we are not biologically meant to have to respond to something like COVID for such a long time. So these feelings of exhaustion and languishing. Burnout. Wear. Drain. All of the things you may be experiencing.

They are normal.[5,6]

And many of us are feeling them.

Getting to the Heart of the Matter

Now, while much of my fatigue is likely caused by this overactivated "fight or flight" response, I know that a lot of it also stems from a project that I have worked on over the last couple of years.

A project that was, in large part, the inspiration for this book.

A project that I have led as part of the United States' (U.S.) response to COVID.

Over the course of this pandemic, it has taken up most of my time and, if I am being honest, much of my being.

I gave all of myself to this project. I mean, we were quarantining in COVID, right? So how else should I have been spending my time? All joking aside, though, it has been all consuming.

As I think back over the course of 2020 and 2021, I think I experienced something incredibly profound. I think I gave so much to this project that I lost a little bit of myself. I made sacrifices for this project: My health, my personal time, and put off things that I had been wanting to do (like reading non-work-related books). All in order to make enough space for this project to take up residence in my life.

I missed walks with my dog, Bear.

I missed eating meals with my husband.

I remember when my wedding anniversary was approaching and I *had* to tell my team that I would not be working that night so that I could spend the evening with my husband. He cooked us dinner—alone—because I did not have the time to join him. And while it was an evening that took place amidst so much stress and turmoil, it was an evening I still think about today. We hung out at home (because we could not go anywhere). It was snowing outside. And the meal was so delicious. The memories of that anniversary celebration are still with me today.

As are the boundaries I needed to set to be able to have those memories.

I know I am painting a pretty negative picture of this time for me but despite all the negative, this project—and all of the experiences that came with it—have also been incredible.

This project is one that I am honored to have been a part of, and one of which I am immensely proud. As a health communicator, these opportunities—to be part of something so vital, so huge, so impactful for people suffering during a global crisis—come once in a lifetime. IF EVER. I am deeply aware of this and thankful for what this project has meant to me and to others and for being able to do this kind of work during this time.

In telling you all of this, I am not trying to gain your sympathy or pity. Or impress you. It is not about the emotion of it all.

It is more about processing the sheer reality of how big COVID has been for us as a global community and how much space it has taken up in each of our lives. How much space it has taken up in my life personally. Which is something that I think I am still in the process of understanding.

COVID Has Amplified EVERYTHING: The Good, the Bad, and the Ugly

During COVID, our worlds (home, work, friends, physical, spiritual, emotional) have all run together. The boundaries of going to work, going to the gym, seeing a friend for dinner, going on a business trip, or taking a vacation have all been removed and the edges of everything have blurred.

This has amplified things, making the everyday annoyances, stressors, and triggers stronger, more complex, more overwhelming, more ... everything.

It is like COVID has put our lives, experiences, and emotions in a Petri dish where they have grown bigger, stronger, and faster—under just the right conditions.

This is something I have been thinking about for a while now.

I have seen people making BIG life decisions in COVID: They have purchased or sold a home, changed careers, quit jobs, ended relationships, started new ones, gotten pregnant, had babies, moved cities, etc.

How many of you know someone (maybe yourself) who has gotten divorced in COVID? I have known of a number of people who have, and I have heard about the stories of many more.

In fact, early in the pandemic, there were data that signaled increases in break-ups and divorce rates. One British law firm, Stewarts, reported a 122% increase in inquiries in divorce proceedings between July and October of 2020, compared with the same time period in 2019. In the U.S., there was a reported 34% increase in sales of basic divorce agreements at a leading legal contract-creation website and similar patterns have also been seen in both China and Sweden.[7]

I have wondered a lot about decision-making in COVID. Should we be making these big decisions in this kind of situation? Or should we be holding off?

And if we hold off, how long do we wait? If COVID stays with us forever, we cannot just stop making decisions and taking steps forward. But how do we know we are making the right decision(s) when the context for that decision is so unusual and stressful?

I have questioned whether COVID is, in fact, that Petri dish? Does it make things bigger and more amplified than they would otherwise be? Or does it really just shine a light on things that were always there that maybe we never took the time to stop and really examine? And if we removed COVID, would everything just go back to the way it was or would we still look at everything around us differently?

I have had this conversation with a lot of people over the course of the pandemic. Most people I have spoken with have agreed that COVID is more the "light" than the "Petri dish"—that it has just brought to the forefront things that were already there, but that we had not paid attention to previously.

But it is not just issues related to buying or selling a house or getting a divorce that COVID have amplified. COVID has also shined a light on those disparities in people's experiences I started to discuss earlier (and that we will get into more throughout this book)—the need to choose between one's health and one's economic situation; the increased risk of infection and death because of the kind of job one has or where one lives; and the substantial economic impact that has been happening disproportionately as a result of getting sick, being uninsured, and being unable to work.

So I think that is right. COVID is a light. But if COVID is the "light," is it a light for just the bad stuff? Or does it also illuminate the good things?

Data from about a year into the pandemic suggests it does both. In addition to the negative impacts that the pandemic has had on social connections, health and well-being, and economic security, multiple studies, including one by the Pew Research Center, have found that there have also been several "silver linings." These have included things like a renewed emphasis on and appreciation for relationships, an increase in free time to do other things (e.g., read, knit, cook, and work out), and coming together (even if only virtually) to help each other (e.g., making masks and bringing food to people who could not leave their homes).[8,9,10]

And those signals of increased divorces that we saw early in the pandemic? Well, it did not exactly turn out as one might have thought. Data from early 2021 contradict these early trends, finding that, in fact, in 2020 there were only 191,053 divorces, compared to the approximate 1 million divorces in 2019.[11]

Thus, it would seem that COVID amplifies both the good and the bad.

So, how does all of this relate to my experience? How has the "light" that is COVID impacted my life? I would say the same holds true for me—it has illuminated both the bad and the good.

With all the hard parts of this experience have also come so many positive things. Professionally, I have gotten to work with an amazing team. I have learned so much throughout the process. I have had my patience and will tested along the way but I have also grown as a manager and as a communicator. I have pushed myself to do more than I have ever done before—and ever thought possible. My team and I accomplished an amazing amount of work in such a short period of time. And we were successful. We developed an award-winning campaign that has had a measured positive impact on those who needed it most.

There were also many personal silver linings. For every meal I missed with my husband, we found new ways to carve out time to connect. We had stay-at-home date nights. I prioritized our morning walks with him and Bear. We learned new activities such as playing chess and mountain biking. We also tried to Zoom or FaceTime more with family and friends whom we could not see in-person.

Finally, I will always carry with me the profound joy that came from being able to spend almost every day over the course of the pandemic with Bear, until he passed away during the writing of this book. Bear was a gift to us in COVID. He kept us on a schedule and made us get up and walk every day. He helped break up the seemingly endless days of meetings, Zoom calls, and deadlines. He saved us in so many ways from the monotony and negative effects of COVID, and I will always be grateful that we had this much time together at what would eventually become the end of his life.

As is often the case with things in life, the hard things can make the good things that much sweeter.

COVID has done that for me in many ways, and it likely has done the same for you.

But, How Are You Really?

So by now, you are saying, just get to the point already: What is this project you keep talking about that has had such a profound effect on you during COVID?

Well, I have had the chance to work with the CDC Foundation and the Centers for Disease Control and Prevention (CDC) to develop a mental health, coping, and resilience campaign called *How Right Now*[12] (or *Que Hacer Ahora*,[13] in Spanish; for the purpose of the discussion in this book, I will use *How Right Now* to refer to the campaign).

Yes. A mental health and coping communication campaign. In COVID.

I have spent the last two years working with my team and my clients at CDC and the CDC Foundation to build and run a campaign that aims to take the real experiences and feelings of people living through COVID and turn those into actionable messages to help improve coping and resilience. We have spent the last two years asking the question,

But, really, how are you?

To build *How Right Now*, my team and I spent months talking with and hearing from people about their struggles, worries, and fears during COVID. People who have had friends and family die. People who have been caretakers themselves and worried about getting sick or getting their loved ones sick. People who have been depressed, anxious, angry, and lonely. People who have been worried about their finances. People who have been experiencing violence at home during quarantine. People who have struggled to know how to keep their kids safe. People who have just wanted to get back to "normal" but have not yet felt safe to do so.

Despite all of these negative experiences, however, we also heard stories of hope. Stories of people and communities coping—despite such hard times and in the face of such adversity. These same people have talked about how "the sun will come out tomorrow" and that "tomorrow is a new day." They have remained hopeful—maybe not because they truly have felt this way all the time, but because they have recognized that they need to be hopeful in order to get through this time. They have exhibited incredible resiliency.

I have had the unique opportunity to listen to all these other experiences, in the midst of my own. I have been able to listen to "their pandemic stories."

Context Matters

One of the things I have learned from listening to the "pandemic stories" of others is how much context has mattered in this pandemic.

Context has mattered because it has influenced how each of us has experienced the pandemic. It has determined things such as financial security, health, safety, sickness, and death. It also has impacted our views of and hopes for the future. It has influenced how we have felt throughout this time. And it has been a contributing factor to our "chronic stress" and our "fatigue."

This is, in part, because of the disparities that different groups have experienced—and have been experiencing—in and before COVID. We have just begun to scratch the surface of this topic in this chapter and we will delve into it more throughout the course of this book. However, context also matters because of something we have not yet mentioned—that is, the wild media environment in which we have been experiencing this pandemic. Our current media environment delivers updates moment-by-moment and has resulted in exposure to LOTS of new information, data, findings, threats, and ways to protect ourselves every day over the course of the past several years. *(Do you remember when we were not sure if COVID was transmissible via surfaces? It seems like such a long time ago when we were having that debate. For the record, it turns out that, no, COVID is not transmissible via surfaces.)*

As well, our current media environment enables and promulgates confusing, downright inaccurate, and politically motivated information. *(Remember ALL THE TIMES we have debated if masks would help curb the spread of COVID? And yes, for the record, masks do work.)*

This communication environment has contributed to our "chronic stress" because many of these updates and much of the information we have been exposed to have not been happy. Most of them have had to do with death, sickness, negative outlooks for the future, economic turmoil, and political controversy. Really, much of the information that has been out there over the past several years has been devastating.

It has also contributed to our "fatigue" as we are tasked with managing such information overload and making sense of it. What is most up-to-date and accurate has not always been clear. What information could be trusted has, at times, been confusing. And whom to believe has shifted, depending on the day, the message, and the communication channel used.

As a result, context has played an important role in determining the information that we have had access to, what we have thought and believed about the pandemic, and how we have acted and reacted as a result. It has shaped our beliefs about how the pandemic has been handled, whether or not to wear masks, our decisions about whether to get vaccinated, and whom we trust for such information.

We each have an individual pandemic story to tell, and it is solidly based in the context of our own lives. Those lives—and those stories—reflect our very personal beliefs and perspectives. Our contexts.

These things matter. The messages and counter-messages we see matter. Communication matters.

Context has mattered.

My hope is that this book will be a start to—and only a part of—a broader conversation that will happen about the vital role that context plays in pandemic communication.

So, What Comes Next?

This brings us to the part of the book where I tell you a little bit about what you should expect to read in the coming pages.

Although I started writing this book to process my own experiences, in writing it, I have expanded it to include the experiences of others and to situate those experiences in the context of this pandemic as well as ones that have come before it.

Thus far, I have shared a little bit about my personal experiences in COVID: What I have gone through and what I have been thinking about related to how COVID has impacted me and the people I know. I also have started to share a little bit about what others have gone through and experienced, what some of the data say, and what some of the silver linings have been. Finally, I have begun to discuss how our media and communication environment plays a role in shaping our experiences in this pandemic.

Throughout the rest of this book, I will talk more about these things. I will share more about people's differing experiences and the differences between them. I will talk about these experiences in the context of social determinants of health and how the pandemic has exacerbated disruptions to those determinants.

I will offer thoughts on approaches and frameworks that guide pandemic and emergency responses generally but will also pull from crisis communication strategies in the private sector to examine what is working and what is not working in today's context.

I will examine broadly the communication environment in which we have been responding to this pandemic and discuss the messaging that we have been exposed to during this time as a result. I will talk about developing a campaign as part of the response to the pandemic, what other campaigns have rolled out during COVID, and what it has been like to build and lead a team completely remotely in this context.

I will talk about risk perception Trust. Mis- and disinformation. Disparities. Messaging. Echo chambers. And so much more.

I will discuss the pandemic experiences of teachers. Of older adults. Of caregivers. Of people who experience homelessness. Of essential workers. Of healthcare workers. Of racial and ethnic communities. Of LGBTQIA communities. Of refugees and migrant populations. Among others.

Finally, I will summarize what I think are some of the lessons learned from this pandemic and what we need to do better to prepare for the next one. I end with *my vision* for the future of pandemic communication.

As we move through the following chapters, we will touch on myriad aspects of pandemics and health communication. Each topic we will discuss is grounded in data and evidence but is also anchored by anecdotes from my own—and others'—personal experiences.

We begin with a brief history of pandemic communication. Chapter 2 provides a brief overview of the concepts of pandemics, epidemics, and outbreaks and the differences between them. It then highlights a number of examples of pandemics, including how they originated, the death tolls, and the communication strategies that have been employed to address each. Specifically, we will look at the influenza pandemic of 1918, HIV/AIDS, H1N1, Ebola, and Zika.

This chapter helps set the stage for all the other chapters in this book by making the case that COVID is not unique. There are unique aspects to the COVID pandemic, for sure, but the reality is that we have been dealing with outbreaks, epidemics, and pandemics throughout the history of humankind—and almost annually in my adult lifetime. COVID is just one pandemic in a long line of other pandemics that have emerged over the last two decades.

It also helps makes the case that communication has always been a part of—and has had a role to play in—the responses to these pandemics. Understanding what has been done to support and respond to each of these prior ones may help us understand what and why we did what we did in this pandemic.

Following this chapter, we begin to look at the dimensions of crisis and emergency response communication, with a particular focus on pandemic response communication. Specifically, Chapter 3 explores CDC's Crisis and Emergency Risk Communication (CERC) framework, which aims to help practitioners and leaders communicate effectively during emergencies. We will unpack this program as one possible way of understanding the communication approaches and strategies that have been used in this pandemic. We will also examine approaches used in the private sector and discuss a bit about how people process risk.

This chapter will help us understand some of the theories, frameworks, and approaches that guide emergency, crisis, and pandemic responses. In doing so, it will provide a foundation for the other topics that we will discuss throughout the rest of the book.

From there, we will explore the unique communication environment in which our response to COVID has unfolded and how this environment has been challenging for pandemic communicators. The unique aspects of COVID (e.g., its duration) were related, to some extent, to the very nature of the virus we were combatting. However, they were also exacerbated by our media and communication environment, which is driven by dramatic headlines, eyeballs, and clicks, and plagued by the pervasive misinformation and falsehoods that circulate widely today. Chapter 4 will review these topics.

Following our discussion of our contemporary communication environment, we will explore how this pandemic has unfolded and the messaging that has accompanied each phase. In Chapter 5, we will look at several phases of messaging: The identification of the virus, quarantine and social distancing, mask-wearing, phased reopening, the vaccine rollout, revisiting the need for masks, and new variants and boosters. Across each of these, we will explore what the key issues were and how the messaging shifted.

This chapter will help elucidate how much messaging we have been exposed to about the pandemic over the past several years. It will be useful to understand what has happened and when, how the messaging has reflected what was going on at the time, and how some of the messaging has been unclear and confusing. It is also useful because, as our memories begin to fade about aspects of this pandemic, this chapter may act as a reminder and chronicle of this time.

From there, we will move on to discuss the pandemic experiences of various communities in more depth. In Chapter 6, we will look at what different groups like teachers, youth and young adults, essential workers, the LGBTQIA community, farm and migrant workers, people experiencing homelessness, and healthcare workers have been through over the course of the pandemic. As I mentioned earlier in this chapter, COVID has impacted all of us, but not in the same way; therefore, it is critical to document and discuss these experiences in order to better understand the true impact of the pandemic across communities.

Following this exploration of the unique experiences of different communities, I want to talk more about how the pandemic has brought to light and exacerbated existing racial, social, structural, and economic inequalities. These challenges, which have existed long before COVID, have made it harder for some people to be able to cope with the pandemic, to stay safe and healthy, to be financially secure, and to be hopeful for the future.

To this end, Chapter 7 begins with a deeper assessment of the disparate impact of the pandemic on racial and ethnic communities. It examines how these communities' experiences in COVID have been particularly difficult, but also not necessarily new. Finally, it introduces and reviews the "Social Determinants of Health" framework (which looks at the economic and social conditions that influence individual and community health and well-being) as a lens through which to understand these varying and uneven experiences.

Building on this discussion, I want to spend some time talking about the numerous communication campaigns and initiatives that were rolled out during the pandemic (including my own). Whether to address awareness of the virus itself, the need to wear masks and socially distance, support the roll out of the vaccine, or provide mental health and emotional well-being support, we have seen many different types of campaigns and messaging disseminated throughout this pandemic.

To this end, Chapter 8 begins with a review of my own experience working on *How Right Now* and discusses how the campaign was developed, implemented, and some early evaluation findings. It then reviews other campaigns (such as *#AloneTogether*, the *#SafeHands Challenge*, and *Mask Up America*) that have been implemented here in the U.S. as well as around the globe. It also tackles the #StopAsianHate movement that started as a response to the hate crimes that have ensued against people of Asian and Pacific Islander descent amidst COVID. Understanding what messages were being delivered and what each campaign was attempting to address is critical to better understanding what has been done, what has worked well, and what could be done better for future pandemics.

Related to this, and because of my personal experience working on a communication campaign in support of and in response to the pandemic, I also want to talk a little bit about what it was like to develop such a campaign and lead a team during this time. The team I had the privilege to work with to develop *How Right Now* can only be called "magic"—truly—so it is worth unpacking a little bit about what that experience was like and what worked so well. As part of this, in Chapter 9, we will also look at what the literature tells us are best practices for team building and management. My hope in talking about team building during this time—as well as more generally—is that I may offer some guidance and approaches that may be helpful to others who are doing similar work now and in the future.

Finally, this book concludes with a summary of observations and lessons learned from across the topics I have covered over the prior nine chapters. And based on these, I propose a vision—my vision—for the future of pandemic communication. To do this, in Chapter 10, I lay out a set of identified challenges, proposed goals, and necessary strategies that I think are needed to do better in future pandemics. My hope is that this may be helpful to others who are working in this area and who have struggled over the course of this pandemic so that all of us can be more effective in the future.

Conclusion

Sometimes, as communicators, we work on topics that are interesting but with which we have no direct, personal experience. COVID, however, despite our differing experiences with it, has touched us all. We can all answer that singular question about where we were when the pandemic was first declared. We all have stories about what it was like when we went into lockdown. We have all been touched by this moment in our history.

This is why I set out to write this book. To document what it has been like. To process what it has meant. To juxtapose the universality of COVID with its disparate nature. To think about what this means in the context of pandemic communication. And, finally, to suggest some things that I think need to be addressed to do a better job next time.

I began this chapter—and began writing this book—to help me understand what the pandemic has meant to me. To process what I have been through. So, how am I doing? Am I ok?

The short answers are, "Ok." "Yes."

The more complicated answer is that I am still sorting it all out. I thought when I started writing this book that we would be through this. That everything would be "back to normal" by now. But we are still dealing with COVID. We are still *in it* as I write these words.

Yes, there are glimmers of hope. Yes, we are starting to see signals of "normal life" returning.

And that feels awesome.

Nevertheless, we still have a long way to go. Even if COVID is "ending" and in fact, becomes "endemic" (we will talk more about that in the next chapter), we have a lot of work to do to get better.

Be better.

Do better.

The disparities. The racism. The systemic issues that impact people's ability to thrive. Those things have been with us and will continue to be with us. We cannot forget about them just because we can go to restaurants again.

We also will be facing the longtail outcomes of this pandemic well into the future. The mental health impacts. The financial impacts. These do not go away just because the virus has lessened. We will need to continue to address these issues.

Finally, the issue of mis- and disinformation is critical. It is a major threat to our health, safety, and way of life. And it is not going to go away just because COVID ends or subsidies. It will require a long-term substantial effort in order to successfully address this threat.

We cannot forget about all of these things. We need to remember.

So we will see how things progress.

For now, I want to talk about what we have been through, what we have learned, and what we should hope for for the future.

I have thought through a lot of this and I hope that what follows is informative to you, thought-provoking, and that you may gain new skills or knowledge that can be helpful to you in your work.

Most importantly, maybe this book will not just be cathartic for me. Maybe it also will help you process your own experiences from these last couple of years.

At its core, this is *my* pandemic story, but I hope it may help you with yours.

Chapter 2

A Brief History of Pandemic Communication

Normal led to this.

—Ed Yong

In the spring of 2022, I was speaking at an event focused on women, innovation, and entrepreneurship. It was an amazing lineup of strong, smart, and successful women. One of the panels included this incredible speaker: She was a financial investor in women-owned start-up businesses. She was fierce. And powerful. She was amazing.

And then she said something that surprised me. She said that we could never have predicted COVID.

Now, I understand the point she was trying to make. For many, COVID was unexpected. And certainly, the virus itself was novel.

But I can tell you this: We could predict COVID. We did predict COVID. We just did not listen.

The world of public health has been tracking disease spread since the field's earliest days. Viral infections, outbreaks, epidemics, and pandemics are not new. Yes, as I have already stated, the particular circumstances of COVID may be unique, but the emergence of COVID was inevitable.

DOI: 10.4324/9781003267522-2

Now, that does not make what people have gone through as a result of COVID any less tragic, challenging, or substantial. As was discussed in the Introduction, COVID has been simultaneously universal and unique. We all have had to socially distance, wear masks at some point, make the decision to get vaccinated (or not), and struggle with the idea of returning to in-person events, work, or school. The disruptions to our everyday lives caused by COVID have not been like anything we have experienced before. And all of these things have touched all of us in some way.

However, not all of us have experienced these things in exactly the same way. Some of us live in houses with enough space to accommodate remote work and school comfortably. Others do not. Some of us have not had to worry about losing our jobs and could make the transition to remote work easily. Others have not. Some of us have had to worry about having to go to work and possibly getting sick. Others have not. Some of us have struggled more with the isolation and separation. Others have flourished.

Yet, while COVID has been both universal and unique, it is important to keep in mind that it is, in fact, not special. It is not the first pandemic we have ever experienced—neither in our own lived history nor the history of humankind—and it will certainly not be our last.

In fact, we should not be shocked by the emergence of this pandemic. COVID is just one of the many pandemics that we have faced as a species over the course of history. And in *just my adult lifetime*, it is only one of the multiple pandemics that we have experienced.

It is also not the first pandemic to use certain types of mitigation strategies, like mask-wearing. Yes, this has been done before. As well, communication about pandemics is not new—some of the methods and channels may be new, yes, but the fundamental act of communicating through a pandemic is not.

Exploring this history a bit is important as we consider the COVID pandemic specifically, as it will allow us to place this experience in a larger context of how disease and infection spread has emerged, been managed, and communicated historically here in the U.S. and around the world.

This will be the focus of this chapter.

Outbreaks. Epidemics. And Pandemics. Oh My!

Before we begin to unpack this brief history of recent population-level infections, it is important to talk a little bit about what we mean when we say the word, "pandemic," and what the difference is between a "pandemic", an "outbreak", and an "epidemic."

As humans, we live with certain levels of all sorts of diseases at any given time. These differ by community and region, and they differ by their level of circulation. It is exactly these *levels of disease* that determine what is an "outbreak," what is an "epidemic," and what is a "pandemic."

So, what are the differences?

The baseline level of a disease in a community is called the endemic level, as in, it is endemic, or specific, to that community.[14] When a disease becomes endemic, it means that the disease is always present at a baseline level. It is not down to zero and there are still observable cases. As Dr. Isaac Weisfuse, epidemiologist and adjunct professor in Cornell University's Master of Public Health program, said,

> *Endemic means that the disease or infection reached a steady state where it doesn't cause large outbreaks but it still circulates, causing individual cases.*[15]

Remember the conclusion to the last chapter? Where I mentioned COVID becoming "endemic?" At the time of the writing of this book, we have been hearing more and more about COVID becoming endemic. What that means is that COVID may get to place where it is still with us and is still infecting people. It will never fully disappear, but it is no longer causing large outbreaks.

Occasionally, the amount of disease in a community rises above the endemic level. When this happens, there are several heightened levels of disease that can occur. The three main ones are "outbreaks," "epidemics," and "pandemics."[16] We will address each of these, in turn, below.

Outbreaks, Defined

The first level is "outbreak," which CDC defines as,

> *An increase, often sudden, in the number of cases of a disease above what is normally expected within a more limited geographic area.*[17]

The words, "limited geographic area," may seem vague and undefined but that is because a "limited geographic area" can really mean any small location, for instance a daycare or a small geographic area. The point with "outbreaks" is that there is a noticeable uptick in the number of cases of a disease within that smaller defined area.[18]

Epidemics, Defined

After "outbreak" comes "epidemic." An epidemic is similar to an outbreak in that it also refers to an uptick in cases of a disease above what is normally expected within a defined area.[19,20] However, there are several differences between the two.

First, while outbreaks usually occur in smaller areas, epidemics usually happen across larger geographic areas. The occurrence of an epidemic also means that the disease has begun to spread more rapidly.[21] Finally, it is important to note that epidemics can also refer to both infectious and non-infectious diseases (for example, it can refer to both polio and smoking, respectively).[22,23] For the purposes of this chapter and this book, when we talk about the spread of disease, we are referring to the spread of infectious diseases.

Pandemics, Defined

While outbreaks occur in smaller areas and epidemics are identified when an outbreak spreads more swiftly to a larger geographical area, pandemics are declared when the epidemic spreads to an even wider area. According to the International Epidemiological Association's (IEA) *Dictionary of Epidemiology*, a pandemic is defined as,

> *An epidemic occurring worldwide, or over a very wide area, crossing international boundaries and usually affecting a large number of people.*[24]

Or as CDC notes,

> *A pandemic refers to an epidemic that has spread over several countries or continents, usually affecting a large number of people.*[25]

Declaring something a pandemic is not a random process. Rather, this determination is made by the World Health Organization (WHO) based on how a disease spreads across six phases.[26]

Phase 1 is where viruses are circulating among animal populations and have not been shown to transmit to human beings. In this phase, there is only a minimal threat and perceived risk of a virus turning into a pandemic.

In *Phase 2*, a new animal virus begins to circulate more broadly amongst animal populations and has also now been transmitted to humans. This transmission between animals and humans can happen in a number of ways:[27]

- Through direct contact with the saliva, blood, urine, mucus, feces, or other bodily fluids of an infected animal;
- Through indirect contact with areas, objects, or surfaces that are contaminated with germs from infected animals;

- Carried by a vector such as a tick or insect;
- Through consumption of contaminated food, e.g., drinking unpasteurized (or raw) milk, eating undercooked meat or eggs, or eating raw fruits and vegetables that are contaminated with feces from an infected animal;
- Through consumption of contaminated water, e.g., by drinking or coming in contact with water contaminated with feces from an infected animal.

When a virus transmits from an animal population to humans, the disease is considered a new zoonosis[28] and is considered a possible threat for a pandemic.

Phase 3 is where the new zoonotic disease has caused infections in a small number of people but transmission is still primarily between animals and humans and the risk of human-to-human transmission remains low. In this phase, the new zoonosis is unlikely to cause a pandemic.

It is in *Phase 4* where increased human-to-human transmission of the new virus begins to be seen, with outbreaks experienced in certain communities. Once this kind of transmission among humans is seen, there is a higher risk of a pandemic developing.

In *Phase 5*, human-to-human transmission of the virus has now crossed geographic borders so the infection exists in at least two countries within a WHO region. The WHO has identified six regions of the world, and when a virus spreads between two countries within one of those regions, the virus is considered to have advanced to Phase 5. At this point, the WHO considers a global pandemic inevitable.

Finally, in *Phase 6*, the new virus now exists in at least one additional country within another WHO region. This is known as the pandemic phase and signals that a global pandemic is occurring.[29]

A Walk Down Pandemic Memory Lane

Now that we have a better understanding of the differences between an outbreak, an epidemic, and a pandemic—and how something becomes a pandemic—we can take a look back at several of the more impactful ones that have plagued our global society.[30]

And the headline is this: Pandemics are not new.

We have been dealing with these for more than a hundred years now. Yes, progress has been made in responding to them. The advent of antibiotics and vaccines has helped combat the emergence of infectious diseases and control their spread. However, as viruses continue to evolve and become antibiotic-resistant, they become harder and harder to prevent and treat.

So it is no wonder that COVID emerged *and* we should expect to experience other pandemics in the future.

Understanding the past is critical to understanding our present—and planning for the future. Which makes it worth our time to look at some of the recent outbreaks, epidemics, and pandemics that we have been through.

This is not a book on epidemiology though, rather it is a book about pandemic communication. Therefore, a full history of pandemics is not warranted here. Moreover in order to contextualize our discussion about *communicating through the COVID pandemic*, it is important to consider not just the pandemics themselves, but also the communication strategies that have been used to ameliorate them. So we will review some of the more recent and impactful pandemics that have occurred *and* their corresponding communication strategies.

To do this—and to give you a good sense of the kinds of infectious diseases our world has been grappling with over *just* the last 20 years or so—I have curated a list of some of the worst and most well-known ones and describe key elements of each.

So let's begin. I want to start with an older one though. One that has recently been discussed more due, in large part, to some of the similarities that it has to COVID. That is the 1918 influenza pandemic.

The 1918 Influenza Pandemic[31]

The influenza pandemic of 1918 (also known as Spanish Influenza, Spanish "flu," and the Great Influenza epidemic) was an incredibly deadly global influenza pandemic caused by the H1N1 influenza A virus.

Table 2.1 Quick Facts: 1918 Influenza Pandemic

Disease	Influenza
Virus strain	Strains of influenza A, subtype H1N1
Dates	February 1918–April 1920
Location	Worldwide
Estimated cases	Estimated 500 million between 1918 and 1920
Deaths	Estimated 25–50 million between 1918 and 1920

The name "Spanish flu" is actually a misnomer, as the virus did not originate in Spain. Rather, it has been theorized that the influenza pandemic of 1918 may have originated in the U.S., Europe, or China. In fact, the earliest documented case was from the U.S.

The pandemic lasted from about February 1918 to April 1920 and killed an estimated 50 million people. Within a month of the first case, additional cases were found in France, Germany, and the U.K., and within two years, nearly a third of the global population (an estimated 500 million people) had become infected.

Typical symptoms of the virus included sore throat, headache, and fever. However, many also experienced bacterial pneumonia, which was often the main cause of death. Other reported symptoms included spontaneous mouth and nosebleeds, miscarriages among pregnant people,[1] odd smells or loss of smell altogether, loss of hearing, loss of teeth or hair, delirium, dizziness, insomnia, blurred vision, and impaired color vision.

Although this disease affected everyone, older adults were particularly at-risk. Interestingly enough, however, it also caused unusually high mortality among young adults as it triggered a cytokine storm, ravaging their stronger immune systems.

You can already see some of the similarities between the 1918 influenza pandemic and COVID, and why they have recently been compared. Despite being caused by different viruses, many of the symptoms are similar and the severe health impacts on seemingly healthy, young individuals have happened in both cases—more than a hundred years apart.

However, the similarities do not stop there.

When one considers the communication strategies that were used back in 1918, they look very similar to what we have seen used over the course of the COVID pandemic.

During that time, public health messages highlighted mitigation strategies to help people protect themselves—things like social distancing, covering coughs and sneezes, explaining how germs spread, and how the virus was impacting regular business and personal operations. At the time, posters and newspaper articles were common dissemination channels for these messages. Figures 2.1, 2.2, and 2.3 show examples of news stories and posters that were used to communicate with people about this pandemic.

---

[1] Gender-inclusive obstetric language as documented in: MacKinnon, K.R., Lefkowitz, A., Lorello, G.R., Schrewe, B., Soklaridis, S., and Kuper, A. (2021). Recognizing and re-naming in obstetrics: How do we take better care with language? *Obstetric Medicine*, 14(4), 201–203. https://journals.sagepub.com/doi/full/10.1177/1753495X211060191

Figure 2.1 News Stories About the Pandemic from The Duluth Herald.[32]

Duluth Herald/Duluth News Tribune.

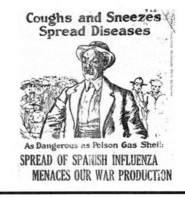

Figure 2.2 Example of a Poster Promoting How Influenza Germs are Spread.[33]

Elizabeth Stephens.

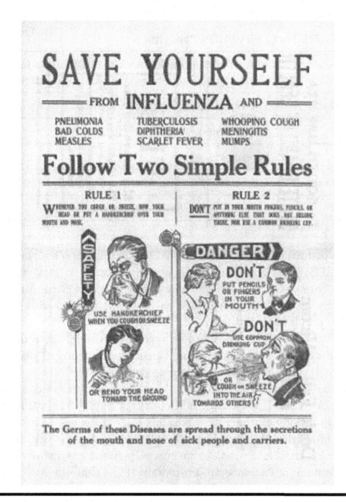

Figure 2.3   Example of a Poster Promoting Prevention Strategies.[34]

Elizabeth Stephens.

Since the 1918 influenza pandemic, there have been numerous other pandemics that we have had to deal with. The next one that I want to discuss is one that has ravaged the world and killed millions of people globally—and is still around today. That is the HIV/AIDS pandemic.

The HIV/AIDS Pandemic[35]

Human immunodeficiency virus (HIV) is the virus that causes acquired immune deficiency syndrome (AIDS). Since its discovery in 1981, it has been commonly referred to as "HIV/AIDS."

Table 2.2 Quick Facts: HIV/AIDS Pandemic

Disease	Human immunodeficiency virus (HIV) is the virus that causes acquired immune deficiency syndrome (AIDS)
Virus strain	The human immunodeficiency virus (HIV)
Dates	1981–present
Location	Worldwide
Estimated cases	Estimated 79 million total cases globally
Deaths	Estimated 36 million total deaths globally

There is perhaps no other disease that has had an impact on human life quite like HIV/AIDS. The Joint United Nations Programme on HIV and AIDS (UNAIDS) estimates that, since the start of the HIV/AIDS pandemic more than 20 years ago, 79.3 million people have become infected with HIV and 36.3 million people have died from AIDS-related illnesses.[36]

HIV/AIDS is widely considered to be a global pandemic, but as the disease has changed over the years and new therapeutics have emerged that help to combat it, it is now identified as "global epidemic" by the WHO. However, given how long this virus has been around, its impact on humanity and health for more than 30 years, and our definition of "pandemic" from earlier in this chapter, I am including it here for discussion.

Exactly how HIV/AIDS originated is still unclear, but the first cases were found among a cluster of people who inject drugs and gay men who began showing symptoms of Pneumocystis pneumonia (PCP) (but who had no known cause of weakened immunity).

Shortly thereafter, there was an unexpected increase in the number of gay men who developed a rare skin cancer called Kaposi's sarcoma (KS). If you recall from our discussion of the definitions of outbreak, epidemic, and pandemic, "noticeable upticks" in disease occurrence is key to identifying the risk of a virus. As a result, and as additional cases of PCP and KS began emerging, CDC was alerted that an outbreak *of something* was occurring (they did not know yet what it was). This started what would become a more than 30-year effort to understand, prevent, and treat HIV/AIDS.

So much has been learned about this virus and so many advancements made during this 30-year period of time. What started out as a disease that was considered to impact only gay men and people who inject drugs is now known to affect *anyone* regardless of sexual orientation, race, ethnicity, gender, age, or where they live.

There was also no effective treatment available early on. Without proper treatment to manage the virus, it traditionally progressed through three main stages of infection:

1. Acute infection which onsets 2–4 weeks after exposure and often is accompanied by influenza-like symptoms;
2. Clinical latency, which typically is characterized by few or no symptoms at the outset but can result in symptoms such as fever, weight loss, gastrointestinal problems, and muscle pains towards the end;
3. Acquired immunodeficiency syndrome, or AIDS, which includes symptoms such as PCP, cachexia (a dramatic loss of skeletal muscle mass and weight loss; also known as "wasting syndrome"), and esophageal candidiasis (infection of the esophagus by Candida albicans).

However, over the years, there have been advancements in antiretroviral therapy and more recently, pre-exposure prophylaxis (PReP), which is medicine people at-risk for contracting HIV take to prevent acquiring it. Ultimately, these developments have meant that contracting HIV is no longer the "death sentence" that it once was. They curb the virus from progressing to AIDS or prevent it altogether, which has led to a shift in focus from "HIV/AIDS" to "HIV" only, as now, people can live with HIV.

Over the years, there have been many communication initiatives that have aimed to raise awareness about HIV and AIDS and educate people about associated risks and prevention strategies. Even with the preventive and therapeutic advancements that have been made, these communication efforts continue today as HIV still effects more than a million people in the U.S.[37] and approximately 38 million people globally.[38]

Several examples of these ongoing communication efforts follow. Figure 2.4 is CDC's first MMWR (Morbidity and Mortality Weekly Report) from 1981 and is considered to be the first major public announcement regarding (what later would become known as) AIDS.

Since then, many different types of advertisements have been run to help promote awareness of HIV/AIDS and emerging prevention and treatment protocols (see Figures 2.5 and 2.6). Notably, Figure 2.6 has been run as a digital ad, which signals the shifts that our communication environment has undergone over the course of the 30 years that public health professionals have been communicating about HIV/AIDS.

While HIV unfortunately continues on, affecting people's lives despite advancements, we have seen several other pandemics emerge alongside of it. One of the more prominent ones we have experienced in the 21st century was the 2009 H1N1 pandemic. We will discuss this one next.

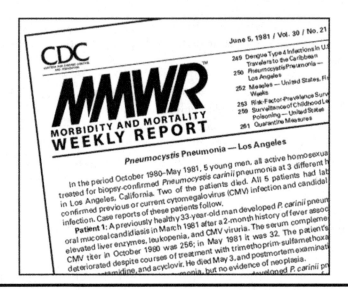

Figure 2.4 CDC's First MMWR from 1981 Regarding (What Later Became Known As) AIDS.[39]

U.S. Department of Health and Human Services/Centers for Disease Control and Prevention.

The 2009 H1N1 Pandemic[40]

Commonly known as "swine flu," H1N1 is a human respiratory infection caused by an influenza strain that started in pigs. The 2009 H1N1 pandemic emerged in the spring of 2009, the first cases of which were detected in the U.S. From there, it spread quickly across the globe.

Table 2.3 Quick Facts: 2009 H1N1 Pandemic

Disease	Influenza
Virus strain	Influenza A virus
Dates	2009–2010
Location	Worldwide
Estimated cases	Estimated 60.8 million between 2009 and 2010
Deaths	Estimated 151,000–575,000 deaths globally between 2009 and 2010

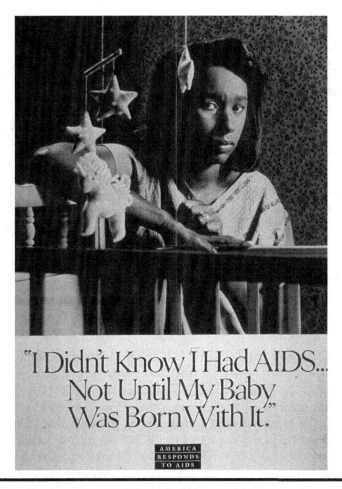

Figure 2.5 HIV/AIDS Advertisement Raising Awareness about Perinatal Transmission of HIV.[41]

Hum Historical/Alamy Stock Photo.

The 2009 H1N1 pandemic holds many similarities to the influenza pandemic of 1918, and some similarities to the COVID pandemic. First, the 2009 H1N1 pandemic was caused by an influenza A virus—just like the 1918 pandemic. Also, similar to the 1918 pandemic, the first cases were detected in the U.S. and spread quickly across the U.S. and the world, affecting anyone (regardless of sexual orientation, race, ethnicity, gender, age, or where they lived), and causing symptoms such as fever, cough, sore throat, chills, and body aches.[42]

Figure 2.6 New York City Department of Health and Mental Hygiene's Play Sure Campaign Advertisement.[43]

Copyright [2023] New York City Department of Health and Mental Hygiene. Reprinted with permission.

And while anyone was susceptible to it, like the influenza pandemic of 1918 and the current COVID pandemic, the 2009 pandemic substantially impacted people younger than 65 years of age (it is estimated that globally 80% of H1N1-related deaths occurred in people younger than 65 years of age).[44]

As well, the communication and messaging strategies that public health professionals used as part of the H1N1 pandemic response were similar to those from both the 1918 and COVID pandemics. Efforts focused on minimizing transmission and promoted mitigation measures such as hand-washing technique, proper cough etiquette, and staying home when sick. Posters and other similar kinds of communication products were developed to disseminate these messages. Figure 2.7 shows a poster from CDC promoting mitigation strategies in response to the H1N1 pandemic.

Figure 2.7 CDC Poster Promoting Mitigation Strategies in Response to the H1N1 Pandemic.[45]

U.S. Department of Health and Human Services/Centers for Disease Control and Prevention.

And just as with the 1918 and COVID pandemics, this pandemic was also not just national—it was global. Figure 2.8 documents an advertisement from the U.K.'s Department of Health's H1N1 campaign across TV, print, and radio.[46]

The similarities between the 1918 pandemic and the H1N1 pandemic of 2009 are uncanny. Similar virus. Similar geographic location where the first cases were documented. We also see similarities between 1918, 2009, and our current COVID pandemic. Similar symptoms. Similar effects on younger people. Similar global impact. And similar communication strategies used.

However, we can also see differences between these pandemics.

One major difference between the 2009 and 1981 pandemics was the sheer impact of the pandemic on sickness and death. You will recall that in 1918, the estimated number of cases was 500 million with approximately 50 million

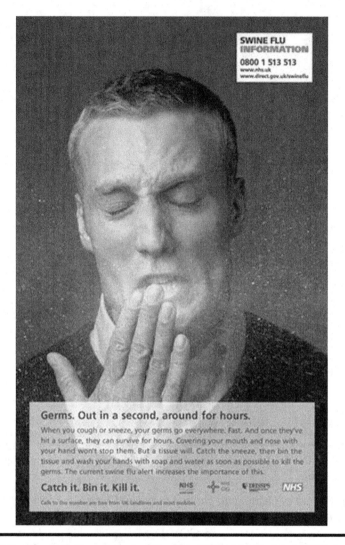

Figure 2.8   The U.K. Department of Health's Public Health Ad about Swine Flu.[47]

United Kingdom National Health Service.

deaths globally. During the 2009 H1N1 pandemic, on the other hand, there was an estimated 60 million people infected between 2009 and 2010 and an estimated 575,000 deaths globally.

That means that H1N1's death rate was *only about 1%* of the death rate of the 1918 pandemic.

The lower morbidity and mortality rates experienced in the H1N1 pandemic are likely due to the rollout of a vaccine that became available during the later pandemic—something that was not available in 1918.

The emergence of a vaccine in 2009 also resulted in a change in the messaging and communication strategies that were being used at the time. These shifted to promote vaccine roll out and uptake (rather than promoting just mitigation strategies like covering coughs and sneezes). This is similar to what we have seen in the COVID pandemic, as the new COVID vaccines rolled out.

This point on the similarity of communication strategies used across pandemics is an important one. And should not be lost on us—similar communication strategies have been used in three different pandemics that have spanned *more than 100 years!*

This is clearly something that needs more discussion, and we will get to that in a bit. However, for the moment, I want to move on from this discussion and turn our attention to another pandemic that we have experienced in our lifetime. One of the scarier ones we have experienced: That is the 2014–2016 Ebola pandemic.

The 2014–2016 Ebola Pandemic[48]

Ebola, otherwise known as Ebola hemorrhagic fever, Ebola Virus Disease (EVD), or ebolavirus, is a virus that causes problems with how blood clots. It can lead to internal bleeding, as blood leaks from small blood vessels in your body. The virus also causes inflammation and tissue damage.

Table 2.4 Quick Facts: 2014–2016 Ebola Pandemic

Disease	Ebola Virus Disease (EVD)
Virus strain	ebolavirus
Dates	2014–2016
Location	Worldwide—but majority of cases were in Africa
Estimated cases	During the 2014–2016 pandemic, there were 28,616 cases in Guinea, Liberia, and Sierra Leone, and an additional 36 cases outside these three countries
Deaths	During the 2014–2016 pandemic, there were 11,310 deaths in Guinea, Liberia, and Sierra Leone, and an additional 15 deaths outside these three countries

It is one of the deadliest viral diseases of which we know.

Ebola was first discovered in 1976 when two consecutive outbreaks occurred in different parts of Central Africa. Initially, public health officials thought those first cases were connected and that an infected person had traveled between the two locations. However, it turned out that the two outbreaks were caused by two genetically distinct viruses: Zaire ebolavirus and Sudan ebolavirus.

This meant that the virus came from two different sources and spread independently to people in each of the affected areas—making this a much bigger and riskier outbreak than previously thought.

Since then, the majority of cases and outbreaks of Ebola have occurred in countries in Africa, but it can affect anyone, anywhere. In fact, the 2014–2016 pandemic started in Guinea but spread quickly to other countries and continents.

Symptoms of Ebola infection may appear anywhere from 2 to 21 days after contact with the virus, with the average onset of symptoms happening between 8 and 10 days. Symptoms typically progress from initial "dry" symptoms (e.g., fever, aches and pains, fatigue) to later-onset "wet" symptoms (e.g., diarrhea, vomiting). Primary signs and symptoms of Ebola may also often include:

■ Sore throat;
■ Loss of appetite;
■ Unexplained hemorrhaging, bleeding, or bruising.[49]

During the 2014–2016 pandemic, a variety of messages and strategies were used to communicate about it. Most were used in the affected countries in Africa, but there was also messaging internationally as the virus spread. Figure 2.9 features an educational poster in Sierra Leone from 2014 that shares information about what Ebola is, how to recognize its signs and symptoms, and how it spreads. Figure 2.10 features a campaign billboard with the slogan "Ebola Must GO" in Monrovia, Liberia from 2015. Finally, as there was quite a bit of news coverage and messaging about the pandemic in the U.S. during this time, Figure 2.11 features one of the front pages of the New York Daily News newspaper during the pandemic.

Thus far, we have covered the 1918 influenza pandemic, HIV/AIDS, H1N1, and Ebola. And yet, there are so many other pandemics that have occurred in our lifetimes that we could talk about.

Smallpox.

Yellow fever.

Cholera.

The Middle East Respiratory Syndrome (MERS) pandemic of 2012.[50]

But we will not have time to discuss all of them here.

Figure 2.9 Educational Poster from Sierra Leone.[51]

Ofeibea Quist-Arcton/NPR.

Figure 2.10 An Ebola Campaign Billboard in Monrovia, Liberia.[52]

ZOOM DOSSO/AFP via Getty Images.

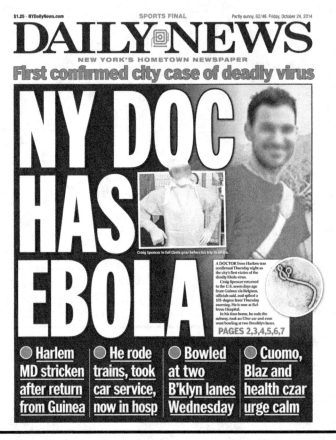

Figure 2.11   News Clipping about Ebola in New York.[53]

New York Daily News/New York Daily News via Getty Images.

I do have one last one that I want to cover in this chapter, however. That is because it is a different kind of pandemic, with a different mode of transmission, and different signs and symptoms. That is the Zika virus pandemic of 2015.

2015 Zika Virus Pandemic[54]

Zika was first identified in Uganda in 1947 in monkeys. About five years later, in 1952, it was identified in humans in the countries of Uganda and Tanzania. Since then, there have been several outbreaks of the virus, with the most recent one being the 2015 Zika pandemic.

Table 2.5 Quick Facts: 2015 Zika Pandemic

Disease	Zika fever
Virus strain	Zika virus
Dates	2015–2016
Location	Worldwide
Estimated cases	During the 2015–2016 pandemic, there were more than 700,000 cases worldwide
Deaths	Deaths from Zika infection are rare and accurate data are hard to find. It is estimated that there were 8 deaths globally during the 2015–2016 pandemic.

The Zika virus can infect anyone and can be transmitted via mosquito bites, through sex, and from a pregnant person to the fetus. It may also be transmitted through blood transfusion (although this is still being confirmed, according to CDC).[55]

The Zika virus tends to cause mild symptoms like fever, rash, headache, and joint or muscle pain[56] but it can have a substantial impact on pregnant people as it can also cause birth defects in their unborn babies.[57] Specifically, these babies are at risk for microcephaly, which is a condition where a baby's head is much smaller than expected due to the brain not developing properly during pregnancy or not growing after birth.[58] There is no known treatment for Zika.

During the 2015 Zika virus pandemic, a variety of communication strategies and tactics were used, both globally and in the U.S., to raise awareness of Zika and promote mitigation methods.[59] Figure 2.12 features airport signage in the U.S. targeted to pregnant people and promoting prevention strategies when traveling to places where the virus was circulating. Figure 2.13 shows a Zika awareness poster from Brazil. And Figure 2.14 shows several creative assets from the CDC Foundation's and CDC's *Detén El Zika (Stop Zika)* campaign.

As we have seen, diseases, germs, and viruses spreading from animals to humans and then from humans to humans is not a new occurrence. There is a long history of these kinds of outbreaks infecting and killing people around the world.

They can originate anywhere. They can have different sources (vector-borne or through contact with animals). They can affect anyone, depending on the virus. They can affect large swaths of people as well as smaller segments of the population. They can cause different kinds of maladies and manifest different types of symptoms (or even no symptoms at all, in some cases). Some can cause high rates

Figure 2.12 Airport Signage in the U.S. about Zika.[60]

Carlo Allegri/Reuters Pictures.

of mortality while others are not as dangerous. Finally, they can last for different lengths of time: Some are shorter in duration while others last for generations.

COVID is just the most recent pandemic we have had and takes its place in a long line of others that have come before it. While the nuances of each of the above-mentioned viruses may be different, it is notable that communication has been a part of every public health pandemic response to them. What is notable about the examples of pandemic messaging and communication that we just reviewed is that they evince how similar the aims, messages, and methods have been across pandemics over the course of recent history.

Maybe the audience changes. Maybe the message changes based on the disease. Maybe the selection of channels changes based on the audience or the time period. Overall, however, all of the communication strategies:

■ Aim to make people aware of the disease;
■ Educate people about the risks;
■ Share prevention strategies and treatment protocols;
■ Encourage behavior change to reduce infection and spread;
■ And use a wide range of communication channels, e.g., news articles/stories, posters, billboards, social media, to reach people with these messages.

The same approach has been used for over 100 years.

Figure 2.13   Zika Awareness Poster in Brazil.[61]

Raquel Medialdea Carrera.

As we close out this chapter, I want to look more closely at this phenomenon—this trend of using similar methods and messages for pandemic communication for decades.

Trends in Pandemic Communication Approaches over the Years

The field of health communication has well established how effective communication can be in supporting awareness, knowledge, attitudes, norms, beliefs, and behaviors in order to help prevent the spread of disease. CDC recognizes this,[62] as do many other health communication and public health researchers and practitioners.[63–71] If we look across the communication approaches used in the aforementioned set of pandemics, some common practices for reaching and communicating about pandemics begin to emerge.

Use of Clear Communication Is Paramount

Providing clear guidance is the best way to help people understand what is going on, what to be aware of, and what they need to do to be safe. Messages like

Figure 2.14   Final Creative from the *Detén El Zika* Campaign in Puerto Rico.[72]

U.S. Department of Health and Human Services/Centers for Disease Control and Prevention.

"Condoms prevent Zika transmission" and the use of imagery to tell people the signs and symptoms of Ebola are examples of clear communication practices used during pandemics.

Frequent and Consistent Communication Is Key

Talking with audiences in ways that consistently communicate the same messages is critical to help avoid confusion. The consistent use of messages like "cover your cough" and "use a condom" have become regular "drumbeat" messages over the years to prevent against certain infectious diseases.

A Robust Set of Tailored Resources That Can Be Used Across Multiple Dissemination Channels Is Needed

To effectively reach people during a pandemic, a robust set of tailored resources needs to be developed and disseminated via multiple channels. This may include press kits with key messages, fact sheets, video testimonials, and clinical resources (to help healthcare providers answer questions from patients). These can be tailored for or by local groups and organizations and adapted for different types of communication channels such as television, Out-of-home (e.g., billboards), radio, social and digital media, print, and events. Examples of this can be seen in 1918 and H1N1 pandemics' posters and news stories, as well as the HIV prevention and *Detén El Zika* campaigns' assets.

These represent key tenets that have traditionally underlain pandemic communication—and they have generally worked to respond to pandemics in the past.

Conclusion

Pandemic communication has always required an understanding of people's lived experiences, the people and voices they trust, and their beliefs, perspectives, and sensitivities about health issues in order to convey information in such a way that it will be heard, attended to, and hopefully believed and followed.

We are living and communicating in a very different environment today, though. One in which we are faced with and influenced by all sorts of new voices and sources of information.

The Internet.

24-hour cable news.

Streaming *everything*.

Social media influencers.

Texting.

Gaming.

TikTok.

These have resulted in fragmented audiences, limited attentions spans, and a plethora of mis- and disinformation. These compete with public health messaging for attention and make this kind of communication challenging—as we have seen in COVID.

These also make this new environment a dynamic one. This means that one message will not work for everyone all the time and for every channel or situation. We need to remain nimble as things change over time. We need to constantly refine what is working and what is not in order to ensure that we are serving communities in the best way possible *in the moment*. For any moment.

Finally, this environment is also one in which context matters perhaps more than ever before. There are important issues related to historical trauma and discrimination that have eroded trust in government and other traditional institutions for decades. These influence what and whom people listen to and believe. So, as I just mentioned, one message disseminated through multiple channels is not enough anymore. We need to *deeply* understand the communities we are seeking to serve and develop communication strategies that address their particular needs.

There is a lot more to discuss about each of these topics—and we will tackle each of them, in turn. Before we can do that, though, we need to first understand some basics. We need to talk a bit about why these approaches have been used. What has historically guided these pandemic communication efforts. What models, frameworks, and tenets are emergency, crisis, and risk communication principles predicated on. And we need to look to both the public and private sectors for this. This will be what we discuss next in Chapter 3.

Dimensions of Crisis and Emergency Response Communication

The secret of crisis management is not good vs. bad,
it's preventing the bad from getting worse.

—*Andy Gilman*

The Space Shuttle Challenger disaster is a vivid memory from my childhood.

I remember the buildup to it. I remember the initial excitement about the launch of the shuttle—Christa McAuliffe was going to be on the shuttle as the first teacher in space. McAuliffe was selected to go to space as part of the National Aeronautics and Space Administration's (NASA) "Teacher in Space" project. Designed to inspire students, honor teachers, and spur interest in mathematics, science, and space exploration, teachers would be selected to go into space as non-astronaut civilians (called "payload specialists") in order to then return to their classrooms and share their experiences with their students.[73]

It was a historic moment.

I remember watching the launch of the Space Shuttle Challenger with my parents. I remember watching as the shuttle began its ascent. And I remember feeling shocked and horrified as, shortly after launch, the space shuttle exploded mid-air, killing all seven crew members. Including McAuliffe.

DOI: 10.4324/9781003267522-3

As an adult, I have other memories of largescale, devasting and life-changing events.

I remember the exact moment when I learned about the attacks on the World Trade Center buildings on September 11, 2001. I remember where I was. I remember what I was doing. I remember watching on television as the plane hit the second tower. I remember going to class that afternoon (I went to school in Canada so classes were not canceled that day), and I remember discussing what had happened and what it was all about.

I also remember when Hurricane Katrina hit the city of New Orleans and the surrounding areas in 2005. I remember seeing on the news all the damage that had been done. The flooding. The evacuations. The rescue efforts. The news about using the Superdome to house people.

Disasters, emergencies, and crises have a way of sticking with us. They are anchors in our memories because of their size and scale and the devastation and tragedy they bring with them. We remember them because of their impact on people and places. And because we are all vulnerable to them.

As a global community, we have experienced so many.[74] I name *just a few* that have affected people here in the U.S. and around the globe below.

The 1970 Huascarán avalanche.

The 1989 Exxon Valdez oil spill.

The 2005 Kashmir earthquake.

The 2008 Sichuan earthquake.

The 2010 Haiti earthquake.

The 2011 Tōhoku earthquake and tsunami in Japan.

The 2012 California wildfires.

The Flint, Michigan water crisis that started in 2014 (and which has not been fully resolved yet).

Hurricane Maria in 2017.

The 2017 California wildfires.

The Australia wildfires of 2019.

The Australian wildfires of 2020.

The 2021 Haiti earthquake.

The 2021 California wildfires.

Dealing with disasters, emergencies, and crises and communicating through them is nothing new. We have been doing this for hundreds of years. As we saw in the last chapter, our ability to respond to pandemic-related emergencies goes hand-in-hand with the use of communication strategies and approaches.

Despite this, the role of pandemic communication (and the importance of it) has not really been something we have talked or thought much about, generally speaking. That is, until COVID happened.

The onset and duration of the COVID pandemic has raised emergency response communication to the forefront of our collective consciousness. We have talked at length over the past several years about how the messaging in COVID has been confusing, or imbalanced, or politically biased. We often talk about the amount and types of mis- and disinformation that have circulated about COVID. And we still talk about who shares what kind of messaging and how impactful it is (or is not).

We talk more about pandemic communication now than I think we ever have before.

It makes sense that we do, though, as there is inherently a symbiotic relationship between pandemic management and communication. In the midst of any crisis, we act differently than we would in a non-crisis situation. We may not recall much of what we hear and see. We may not fully listen to the information that is being shared with us. We may misinterpret information that is not clear to us. Our behaviors may not always be logical ones. We might follow bad examples set by others.[75]

Notably, communication can help address these issues. Communication enables public health practitioners to share accurate and up-to-date information, to disseminate regular and frequent updates, to combat inaccurate or false information, and to use a variety of channels—including working with trusted voices—to do so.

As we mentioned in the last chapter, though, communicating about infectious diseases and pandemics is hard; and it is getting harder as the environment in which we are communicating …

Changes quickly.

Grows more diffuse.

Becomes increasingly curated, niche, and siloed.

Is mobile.

And requires more nuance.

Therefore, we need to be able to navigate this complex space better in order to communicate more effectively. Understanding models of and approaches to emergency, crisis, and risk communication will help provide a foundation in order that we may be able to do this.

Throughout the course of this chapter, this is our aim: To understand the guiding principles of emergency, crisis, and risk communication from both the public and private sectors and how approaches from both can be used to support modern-day pandemic communication efforts.

Some Definitions before We Get Started

Before we go any further though, it is worth spending a little time talking about a couple different concepts that have applicability to our discussion and that will be used throughout this chapter. Those are "emergency response," "crisis communication," and "risk communication."

The concepts of "emergency response," "crisis communication," and "risk communication" are interrelated, and as such are often used interchangeably. This is because "risk communication" is related to "crisis communication," and "crisis communication" is essentially baked into the fabric of "emergency response."[76]

By definition, "emergency response" is:

> *Primarily operational in nature, focusing on support to first responders and transition to immediate recovery.*

For instance, if a hurricane hits, emergency response efforts typically mobilize quickly to evacuate people, find shelter for displaced people, and address the aftermath (e.g., cleaning up and restoring basic services like water and electricity).

"Crisis communication," on the other hand, is:

> *More strategically oriented, with high-level officials primarily focusing on long-term impacts.*[77]

Crisis communication typically tries to address scandals or product or service issues using strategies such as swiftly responding, putting the "victims" first, being transparent about the issue, providing an answer to the problem, and being consistent.

Finally, "risk communication" is:

> *Communication intended to supply audience members with the information they need to make informed, independent judgements about risks to health, safety, and the environment.*[78]

This kind of communication aims to identify the risks posed to humans and the environment, understand and manage them, and communicate with people about them.

These three communication approaches are unique, but there is a synergistic relationship between them. Emergency response is part of crisis communication (in so far as the problem needs to be addressed operationally in some way). Crisis communication is part of emergency response (as in, the problem needs to be skillfully communicated about). Finally, risk communication is related to both (as risks to people and the environment need to be understood, managed, and communicated). This makes the inclusion of all three of these concepts in a discussion of crisis, emergency, and pandemic response communication vital.

Therefore, throughout this chapter, I will use all three of these. I will use them discreetly in places, but I will also blend elements from each and talk about the ideas of "emergency response communication," "risk communication," "crisis communication," and "pandemic response communication," acknowledging how crisis communication, emergency response, and risk communication are inherently linked.

Crisis Communication in the Private Sector

Crises, and the communication approaches used to address them, are phenomena experienced in all fields, not just public health. While the field of public health has been responding to crises (e.g., pandemics, wildfires, floods, contaminated water) for over 200 years,[79] the private sector has dealt with its own share of high-profile and seemingly catastrophic disasters over the years.

In fact, crises in the private sector are *quite* common, and we do not have to look too far to find examples.

We have seen Uber lose 200,000 users in the wake of the #DeleteUber hashtag campaign that ensued when Uber continued its operations despite New York City taxi drivers striking in reaction to then-President Trump's travel ban.[80]

United Airlines lost $800 million in value in just a few hours after a video surfaced of a man being dragged off of a plane, due to the flight being overbooked.[81]

During the pandemic—when more people than ever were online and working remotely—Amazon Web Services (AWS) experienced several major outages to its services that threatened business operations for its clients.[82]

Exercise equipment and media company, Peloton, received severe backlash when its holiday ad campaign (which featured a woman thanking her husband for getting her a Peloton bike) outraged viewers because the woman came across as "terrified" and "trying to please her spouse."[83]

Finally, we are all likely familiar with the data breaches that Facebook (before it was rebranded "Meta") experienced in 2013. And in 2018. Oh, and again, in 2019.[84]

And Meta's own study that found that Instagram fosters feelings of anxiety, depression, and body dysmorphia amongst teen girls.[85]

These are just a few examples of the kinds of crises that private sector companies deal with regularly and frequently. Many other companies and brands (e.g., PepsiCo, Johnson & Johnson, Motrin, Domino's Pizza, DirecTV, and Comcast) have all experienced and had to face crises that have threatened their bottom lines and posed possible threats to their existence.[86]

However, as of the writing of these pages, all of these companies and brands are still around. Yes, they may have taken a financial hit in the moment of their crisis. Maybe even lost some of their market share. And certainly they experienced some reputational damage. But the impacts of these crises have generally been short-term, and the companies have not been completely devastated or ruined by them.

This ability of private sector companies to prepare for, deal with, and come out OK on the other side of crises is seemingly common. And impressive (whether you like it or not). Large companies seem to always be well prepared to weather the "tweetstorms" of angry customers about product malfunctions, service interruptions, and poor experiences.

Because of this, spending some time looking at crisis response and communication in the private sector is vital to any discussion about emergency and pandemic response communication. Therefore, before we jump into discussing public health emergency response communication, I want to examine more closely some approaches and lessons learned from the private sector.

Specifically, there are four examples I want to look at in more detail. These four companies have successfully navigated some of the most well-known crises from over the last 40 years and they are generally regarded as the best. These are Johnson & Johnson, Pepsi Co., American Red Cross, and Kentucky Fried Chicken.[87] The ways in which these brands responded to their crises can tell us a lot about their crisis management strategies and teach us something about how we might approach our own public health crises.

Johnson & Johnson

In 1982, Johnson & Johnson faced a major issue when seven people who had taken the company's over-the-counter painkiller, Tylenol, died from poisoning due to bottle tampering. To address this crisis, Johnson & Johnson took several immediate steps to identify the problem and address it.

They immediately ran advertisements to alert consumers not to take their product. They also stopped production and ordered a national recall. And in just six weeks, they designed the first, triple-lock tamper-resistant container to help prevent something like this from happening again in the future.

Their immediate and transparent response to the crisis helped Tylenol regain its market share. Their focus on the health and safety of consumers instead of profits in the short term helped them regain the trust of their customers, and this led to their continued success in the long term.

Pepsi Co.

In 1993, a Washington state couple claimed that they found a syringe in a bottle of one of Pepsi Co.'s products, Diet Pepsi. In response to the allegation, Pepsi Co. created a video campaign to demonstrate the canning process in an effort to show that such a mistake was simply impossible.

In doing this, the company aimed to be transparent in its communication with consumers. Additionally, by allowing its consumers to take "a-peek-behind-the-curtain" of its production process, Pepsi Co. was able to dispel the allegations and regain consumer trust.

American Red Cross

In 2011—in the early days of social media—an American Red Cross employee posted an inappropriate personal tweet from the organization's account. It read,

> *Ryan found two more 4 bottle packs of Dogfish Head's Midas Touch beer .... when we drink we do it right #gettngslizzerd.*

Instead of ignoring the tweet, the American Red Cross took a humorous approach and posted another tweet saying,

> *We've deleted the rogue tweet but rest assured the Red Cross is sober and we've confiscated the keys.*

By addressing the issue in an authentic way, the American Red Cross managed to successfully handle what could have been an incredibly embarrassing situation. Coincidentally, this also happened to result in successfully securing additional donations in the wake of the issue.

Kentucky Fried Chicken

In 2018, Kentucky Fried Chicken (KFC) experienced what could only be called a "nightmare" situation: Most of KFC's outlets in the United Kingdom (U.K.) and Ireland ran out of chicken!

In response to the outrage from customers, the brand placed a full-page ad in *The Sun* and *Metro* newspapers (leading newspapers in the U.K.) acknowledging their supply chain issues and apologizing for having to close down hundreds of their stores.[88]

The ad also featured a "creative and humorous" visual: An empty chicken bucket with the company's brand name letters rearranged to read, "FCK."[89]

KFC's response was quick, smart, humorous, and on-brand. It helped to address the issue head-on, acknowledged people's frustrations, and stopped the issue from becoming bigger than it was.

These examples demonstrate how the use of effective crisis communication strategies can help address issues, build trust, and maintain credibility in the face of critical situations. Moreover, there are similarities across the approaches employed by all four bands that enabled their success.

First, each brand chose *not to remain silent* in the face of a crisis. In these moments, it is crucial for brands to be aware of what is going on and decide the reputational impact of the crisis and how best to respond. By remaining silent, a brand may come across as detached and disinterested, and this may run counter to the brand's values that it aims to embody. It is exactly *in crises* when it is most important to hold true to a brand's values in order to craft a response that will navigate the issue successfully.

The brands' responses were also *simple*. Each addressed the crisis with a simple message that acknowledged the issue and the steps that were being taken to address it.

As well, each response was *fast*. Relatively speaking, as soon as the crisis happened, all of these brands were quick to decide on and activate a response. To be able to respond quickly, however, means that you have planned ahead, that you have thought through what a response to a crisis might look like, even if you don't know what the crisis will be. Pre-planning in advance of a crisis is critical to being able to respond quickly when something does happen.

All of the responses were also *consistent* and *"on-brand,"* allowing them to respond in a way that aligned with what people knew about them and made sense to their customers and constituents. This also helped to keep their brands front and center, all the while turning attention away from the crisis.

Many of them also used *humor* to address their crisis. Use of humor is a delicate thing, as it does come with the risk of appearing to make light of a serious situation; but the use of humor, in the right context, can help address crises in a way that can rebuild trust with people.

Finally, many of the responses addressed *functional or operational concerns*. That is, they aimed to help consumers better understand how an issue happened and how the brand was fixing that issue. This helped to show how each was addressing the issue and strengthened trust with their customers.

These are all good lessons from the public sector—ones that can be employed, in large part, in response to public health emergencies. Yet, it is important to note here that there are fundamental differences between responding to a chicken shortage and trying to respond to a virus that is threatening people's lives. Therefore, having reviewed lessons from the private sector, I want to now turn our attention to discussing pandemic and emergency response communication approaches next.

But Infectious Disease Doesn't Taste Like Chicken

I think we can all agree on the fact that there are fundamental differences between handling a soda or chicken crisis and responding to a global pandemic.

Not that I am downplaying what it means for a brand to face an issue with its product that directly affects its customer base and bottom line, but at the end of the day, there are differences.

First, most of these private sector crises are not a matter of life or death. Lives are, for the most part, not at stake. As well, private sector issues, while upsetting to customers and impactful to the companies themselves, are often simpler to explain.

Issues such as a chicken shortage or forcefully removing a passenger from a plane are, yes, stressful, concerning, and embarrassing, but they are often easier to discuss with people. Even product tampering, while life-threatening and indeed worrisome, is something that can be communicated about simply.

These issues can also be fleeting.

We see this in several of the examples noted above: Amazon's web services outages, Facebook's constant data breaches, #deleteUber. These issues have occurred, been in the news, and made us ask questions about the aims and ethics of these companies. But then—quite quickly and quietly—they fade from the headlines and join the other things we store in the recesses of our memories, as we move on from them to focus on other things.

All of these aspects of private sector crises make crisis communication in those contexts paramount, but also somewhat easier.

In a pandemic response, however—especially one like COVID—public health practitioners may be facing a new virus that is complicated, unrelenting, dynamic, fast-moving, and ever-changing. This means that it can be hard to explain simply and clearly the science behind it.

It also means that the issue does not go away quickly or quietly. It remains in the news and top-of-mind for most of us. This means that one quick, on-brand response will not cut it. Rather, an ongoing and lengthy response that can address each twist and turn is required.

It is also incredibly depressing to have sickness and death in the headlines all day, every day. This can impact people's emotions and feelings of hope and cause general fatigue as the crisis drags on. So while an ongoing and lengthy response may be needed, it can also mean that people get tired of hearing the same messages, begin to tune them out, and do not attend to them in the same way over time.

Thus, with such a complicated, unrelenting, dynamic, fast-moving, and ever-changing virus, this kind of messaging and the timing of such communication can often appear slow, confusing, incorrect or inaccurate, overly drawn-out, and depressing—even if developed with the best of intentions using best practice approaches.

Pandemic response communication can often be the *antithesis* of what is recommended and needed during a crisis.

- It may be complex (due to the science) when it needs to be simple;
- It may be slow (due to the need to be accurate) when it needs to be fast;
- It may quickly grow irrelevant (due to the dynamic nature of the virus) when it needs to remain relevant;
- And it may appear to be contradictory (again due to the dynamic nature of the virus) when it needs to be steadfast.

So how do we apply best practices from the private sector within the unique context of pandemic communication?

Well, I think we need to understand where and how these strategies can work, and perhaps more importantly, where and how they cannot. And in order to do that, we need to understand the theories, frameworks, and principles that guide response communication.

To this end, throughout the remainder of this chapter, we will explore some select frameworks and constructs from health communication that address the psychology of communication during emergencies and unpack people's perceptions of threat and risk. We will begin by looking at one of the leading examples: CDC's Crisis and Emergency Risk Communication (CERC) framework.

A Review of CDC's Crisis and Emergency Risk Communication Framework

CDC's CERC framework emerged out of a belief that,

> The right message at the right time from the right person can save lives.[90]

CERC draws from lessons learned during past public health emergencies as well as from research from across the fields of public health, psychology, and emergency response and risk communication in order to provide a variety of evidence-based materials, trainings, and tools that may aid public health practitioners in their communication efforts to address emergency and crisis situations.

CERC contends that emergencies unfold over the course of five phases.

Pre-crisis, the time before the onset of the emergency when practitioners should be preparing for an emergency *(remember the idea of planning for a crisis that we learned about from the private sector examples?)*.

The *initial* phase of a response, when there is the greatest confusion, the least amount of information, and when communicating about the risks is paramount *(remember the importance of swift and simple communication from the private sector examples?)*.

Maintenance, when data is collected and analyzed in order to adapt as the crisis evolves *(remember the consistent messaging and logistical approaches used by the private sector brands and companies?)*.

Resolution, when the crisis is finally considered over and the problems that have been encountered are collected and assessed *(remember how creating new product features or providing a glimpse into the production process used by Johnson & Johnson and Pepsi Co, respectively, helped to resolve the issues at-hand?)*.

Finally, *evaluation*, when lessons learned are collected and public health practitioners return to pre-planning in order to get ready for future emergencies *(while this was not addressed in the earlier private sector examples, many brands will do what is called "After Action Reviews" for exactly this purpose)*.[91]

Ultimately, CERC asserts that we are always in one of these five phases and offers a framework by which public health practitioners may understand how emergencies unfold, how to prepare for a crisis, and how to communicate about risk when one hits.[92] Specifically, the six core communication principles of CERC can be found in Box 3.1.

BOX 3.1 THE SIX CORE COMMUNICATION PRINCIPLES OF CERC

Be first. Crises are time-sensitive and require swift communication responses. CERC maintains that the first source of information is often the preferred one.

Be right. Crises require the communication of accurate information, and this includes sharing what is known, what is not known, and what is being done to address those knowledge gaps.

Be credible. Communicating honesty and truthfully are necessities during crises in order to be and remain credible with communities.

Express empathy. Emergency response communication should acknowledge the challenges people are facing and what they are feeling in order to build trust.

Promote action. Crisis communication does not just mean acknowledging experiences, it also means giving people meaningful things to do in response. This can calm anxiety, help restore order, and promote some sense of control.

Show respect. Communication during an emergency should be respectful of the people and situations that such communication is seeking to support and address. CERC maintains that respectful communication enables cooperation.

So if CERC exists, why has the COVID pandemic response felt so messy? So disorganized? And quite frankly, like there was no program or model guiding anything?

Have you felt like this? I know I have.

I think there are multiple reasons why this could be the case. We have already begun to discuss some of them already: The natural complexity of pandemics that makes communication during one hard. The crazy communication environment in which the COVID response has rolled out. Mis- and disinformation. Distrust. Mistrust. Disparities. All of these have contributed to the communication challenges that we have experienced in COVID and we will discuss them in more detail throughout the rest of this book.

However, before we do that, I think that there is one aspect that is important to talk about *here.* That is, the idea of "risk perception," or how differently people perceive risk. Risk communication is central to CERC and pandemic communication, more generally, so it is important to understand how risk perception can impact crisis communication, how people respond to it, and ultimately whether it is successful or not.

The Role of Risk in Pandemic Communication

Public health emergencies can cause a great deal of fear and anxiety, and the aim of crisis communication is to help alleviate these feelings by clarifying the risks and ways to mitigate them. One way to do this is to use clear, simple, and regular communication to clarify and explain the risks and associated mitigation strategies to people. This is the primary tenet of "risk communication" (as noted above).[93] It is also a key aspect of CERC.[94]

Unfortunately, however as we have seen in COVID, people do not always listen OR believe the risk and prevention information that is being shared with them. This has to do, in part, with "risk perception," or how people perceive the risk and the effectiveness of the related mitigation approaches. This, in turn, will influence their decisions about what and whom to believe and what actions to take to protect themselves and others.

One model that aims to understand the risk perception process is the Extended Parallel Processing Method, or EPPM.[95] EPPM posits that when we assess the risk of something, two cognitive processes occur. First, we assess the threat, and second, we assess our ability to respond to that threat. Thus, risky situations are assessed from a problem-solution orientation.

What is the problem?

And what can I do to address the problem?

Within each of these processes, there are two considerations that people take into account. As it relates to *assessing the threat*, people assess their own *susceptibility* to the threat (how likely it is that the threat will affect them) as well as the *severity* of the threat (the magnitude of the impact of the threat if the person is affected). As it relates to *responding to the threat*, people consider their *self-efficacy* to respond (whether they are competent to perform the tasks needed to control the risk) as well as the *response efficacy* (whether they think the actions they can take to control the threat, if employed, will, in fact, successfully control the threat).

It is through this process of threat-response assessment that we are both determining the risk as well as our ability to mitigate that risk in order to make decisions about certain things in our lives. So for example, in the COVID pandemic, if someone believes that they are at-risk of getting infected (*susceptibility*), that they will get sick if infected (*severity*), that there are steps they can take to protect themselves (*self-efficacy*), and that if they take those steps, they will, in fact, be protected (*response efficacy*), they may be more likely to adhere to the measures outlined in traditional pandemic communication messaging.

However, if one of these considerations shifts, people's risk appraisal also shifts. For example, if someone does not see themselves as being susceptible to the virus *at all* (they believe it to be fake) OR if they think that if they catch COVID, they won't get *that* sick (the severity of the infection is low), they may be less fearful overall, and any messaging about the risks of the virus may be less meaningful to them and preventative behaviors may not be adhered to.

Alternatively, if someone does not want to adhere to protective and mitigation measures (e.g., mask-wearing, social distancing, getting vaccinated) (*self-efficacy*) or thinks that doing so will not be effective in preventing infection (*response efficacy*)— even if they fear the virus—messaging having to do with taking preventative actions may be less meaningful to them and therefore, will not be followed.

Risk appraisal is complex and multi-faceted. It becomes even more complicated when we consider how we process risk in today's communication environment.

Risk Assessment in Today's Context

So, it is clear how all four threat-response considerations of EPPM are ideally needed to elicit the right response from people in responding to a pandemic. Someone needs to understand the risk, take it seriously, and believe in the recommended prevention measures, and that they can take the recommended steps to successfully protect themselves in order to effectively reduce their risk. When one or more of these four considerations is missing or our perception of one or more of them is distorted, this weakens the foundation upon which pandemic response communication is predicated.

This threatens positive health outcomes. And it threatens lives.

But as we have been saying, context matters.

In the context of today's communication environment, where people do not have access or listen to the same sources or believe the same information, whom and what people believe differ.

This is, in part, caused by long-standing distrust and mistrust in our systems and institutions, as well as the abundance of mis- and disinformation that exists today.[96] These things can distort our appraisal of risk and threaten effective communication during crises.

In fact, they are chief threats to the public's health today.

For example, we have seen people in this pandemic take the virus seriously, but those same people also do not want to wear masks. They believe that the risk exists and that they are vulnerable to it (*susceptibility*). They believe they may get sick because of it (*severity*), and they even believe they can take steps to control the risk (*self-efficacy*), but they do not believe in the effectiveness of wearing masks (*response efficacy*). Or people do not trust the source through which the mask recommendation is coming and therefore do not trust that the information they are being given about mask-wearing is true (*response efficacy*).

Similarly, we have seen people in this pandemic take the virus seriously, but who also believe in *alternative* mitigation methods like injecting bleach[97] or taking Ivermectin.[98] In this case, they are going through all the same steps in processing the risk of the virus, but they believe that something else will be a more effective response to it. Something else that is actually not effective. Something else that is, in fact, harmful and causing people to die.

So the context for risk appraisal has shifted—and continues to do so. The question *is* what do we do about it? How do we communicate about risk in our current environment? And can the principles of CERC work in this context?

Conclusion

At this point, we have a good sense of the approaches that the private sector uses to address crises. We also understand the main tenets of the CERC framework and how it prioritizes risk as part of its framework. Additionally, we have reviewed what the science tells us about how people process risk and how this process is vital to the success of the pandemic communication process.

Finally, we have also seen how tenuous the risk appraisal process can be and how the outcomes of this process can vary depending on the source(s) and information that are attended to and believed.

We are living and communicating in a complex media environment, though, with 24-hour news, content designed to drive clicks, and social media platforms that incentivize and amplify content with the highest engagement (most of which is not accurate information[99]). Additionally, the misinformation and disinformation that swirl about on the Internet have severely undermined the public health world's messages and recommendations for curbing and controlling sickness and protecting lives.

When one considers these things—our experience in COVID, how messy our current communication environment is, the issues of misinformation, mistrust, and distrust—I wonder ...

Can CERC still work in today's communication environment?

Is it enough?

There is quote by Dr. Steven J. Venette, of the University of Southern Mississippi, that goes,

> *Crisis is a process of transformation where the old system can no longer be maintained.*[100]

If we consider this, and if we consider the six core communication principles of CERC, what does it mean to really "be first" in the age of social media where anyone with a platform and voice can share so-called health information first?

What does it mean to really "be right" when mis- and disinformation abound and lead to the adoption of unsafe health practices that threaten lives?[101–103]

What does it mean to really "be credible" in an environment where "credibility" is not longer just a matter of degrees, expertise, and experience? And when fake news, lies, and conspiracy theories that were once considered comical anecdotes from the dark corners of the Internet or fringe groups have reached higher levels of visibility, awareness, popularity, and belief?

What does it mean to really "show respect" in a world where many communities have been marginalized and discriminated against for generations? Where a majority of people think the healthcare system is rigged against them and that healthcare providers do not have their best interests at heart?[104]

I do not think we know the answers to these questions—at least not all of them and certainly not all of them right now. I do think these questions signal though, how CERC—and perhaps other theories and frameworks—may miss some of the current contextual nuance in their present configurations.

These contextual factors are BIG issues. And we have only just scraped the surface of them here. They are affecting how we go about communicating in crises like the COVID pandemic—and how our messages are received. And it is impacting lives. Therefore, these deserve more discussion, so this is what we will turn our attention to next.

Chapter 4

Pandemic Communication in Our Current Media and Communication Environment

We, the poor, are immune to the coronavirus.

—*Miguel Ángel Barbosa*

There are so many memories that I have—that we likely all have—from this pandemic. I am just starting to unpack mine here in this book. Perhaps you are doing the same in your own life.

Some of these memories are universal—I think we can all recall …

The death.

The dying.

The shuttering of businesses and quarantining.

The panic buying.

Seeing field hospitals being stood up.

Seeing the mass graves fill up with people who had died from COVID.

The introduction of the new COVID vaccine.

The mask-wearing.

DOI: 10.4324/9781003267522-4

The variants.

There are so many others, and we will get to many of them in due time. But there is one moment that stands out to me now, and likely will forever.

It was when, in the early days of the pandemic—in April 2020— then-President Donald Trump took to the podium in the White House briefing room to announce to the American public that he was encouraging his top health officials to study the injection of bleach into the human body as a means of fighting COVID.[105]

I remember that moment so clearly and I recall thinking,

WHHAAATTTT?!?! This is crazy. Inject bleach? To kill a virus? To fight COVID? And how could the President of the United States—one of the most powerful people in the world—publicly suggest something like this?

I thought it was "crazy" because it caused a lot of confusion and uncertainty. I also thought it was "crazy" because of the sheer magnitude of what it meant to have a U.S. President say something like this.

But I truly thought it was "crazy" because following this statement from the then-U.S. President, there were measured increases in calls to U.S. poison control centers[106] and in reports of exposure to cleaning agents.[107] People actually started ingesting bleach because of what the then-President said. Saying this out loud to millions of Americans actually resulted in people getting sick—and not sick from the virus! Sick from trying to use bleach to treat COVID.

And what did the media do in response?

They went wild about it. Reports at the time noted this as "a watershed moment." They called it a seminal point in the history of presidential briefings.[108] It was fodder for them. For their insatiable appetites for sensational content.

Generally speaking, it is well-founded how news media narratives shape societal perceptions of key issues and of ourselves.[109] A U.S. President says something, the media amplifies it, and people listen. A simple message from a powerful messenger with the right platform can have this kind of impact. This singular statement changed the course of the pandemic. And maybe history too.

Remember when then-President Trump tweeted about "the Chinese virus"? In the weeks following that tweet, the number of COVID-related tweets with anti-Asian hashtags increased[110] and coincided with reports of increasing anti-Asian hate crimes.[111–113]

A U.S. President says something, the media amplifies it, and people listen. A simple message from a powerful messenger with the right platform can have this kind of impact.

We now find ourselves into the third year of the pandemic with more than 6 million people dead from COVID globally.[114] This kind of misinformation and misleading supposition is just one example of the crazy communication environment in which we have been living during this time.

We have all seen firsthand the important role the media and communication environment has played in influencing pandemic-related awareness, knowledge, beliefs, and behaviors. I have often wondered, throughout this experience, whether it would have made a difference if we only had one narrative, one story. If it would have made a difference if we had fewer media outlets and voices to amplify, complicate, conflate, and misconstrue things?

Would this have helped control the spread of the virus? Would we have had an easier time getting control of the pandemic? Would it have resulted in more people getting vaccinated? Would more people have taken the recommendation to wear masks seriously? Would fewer people have gotten sick? Would fewer have died? Would there have been less violence? Would we be through it now? Would it be over?

I do not have a crystal ball, so I do not know the answers to all those questions, but I do not think that the answer is as simple as having a single message or voice.

If it were as simple as that, we would not have seen countries like China struggle to contain the virus. And while reports out of China have been generally positive,[115] as I am writing this now, there is a resurgence of the virus in mainland China, where the country is experiencing its worst COVID outbreak since early 2020.[116]

I think a lot of this has to do with trust and how our communication environment contributes, at least in part, to the establishment (or disruption) of trust between governments, institutions, and citizens.

Evidence of this can be seen if we consider the countries of New Zealand and Iceland and how they have approached the pandemic. Both of these countries—despite being on opposite sides of the globe—have generally fared well over the course of the pandemic. They both have some of the lowest deaths per capita and have been commended for their individual responses to the pandemic.

Yet each has used different strategies to control the virus. New Zealand used a "go hard and go early" strategy that included lockdowns, border closings, and quarantining; while Iceland, on the other hand, primarily focused on easy access to testing, mass screening, quarantining, and contact tracing.[117]

So how did these two countries from different parts of the world and using different approaches to respond to COVID each achieve some of the lowest death rates from the virus globally?

Well, what both countries did have in common was high levels of public trust, and this was driven by their use of science to inform policy decisions as well as their use of clear communication.[118]

In the U.S., on the other hand, the confusing and fragmented communication environment in which we live has substantial affected our response to COVID, arguably for the worse. We are already a country with low public trust[119] and this environment has served to erode this further by impacting the information that people have access to. Whom people trust—and whom they do not. Amplifying false claims and therapies and ultimately, impacting the health and well-being of millions of people.

New Zealand and Iceland exemplify just how important clear and consistent communication is in building trust between a government and its people—and how this has made a difference for these countries in combatting COVID. It is not to say that communication is the only reason why a pandemic response will be successful—again, I don't think it is that simple (and, in fact, much of the literature does acknowledge how more work is needed to fully understand what actually comprises a successful pandemic response[120])—but there is one thing I know for sure: Communication certainly has an important role to play in it. Therefore, understanding this role and our current media and communication environment shall be the focus of the rest of this chapter.

So What Is a Media and Communication Environment Anyway?

Before diving into a discussion about our media and communication environment, I want to first define what I mean by "media and communication environment." According to Forbes, it is:

> *The social, mental, and economic environment that a particular medium or technology has engendered.*[121]

From the newspaper you read at your kitchen table in the morning to the smartphone in your pocket, our media and communication environment is the context within which people engage with information. It shapes what we think and how we feel about key issues in our world. It gives meaning to information we consume, which influences our personal perspectives on things; and this, in turn, affects our society, our economy, and our world.

So if this is what a media and communication environment is, let's take a look at what has made our current environment what it is today.

Oh, What a "Media" World We Live In

The media and communication environment we engage in today is like nothing we have ever experienced before.

Forty-plus years ago, did we *even* know we needed news updates 24-hours-a-day? Probably not.

Twenty-plus years ago, could we ever have imagined that our friends' network would be interested in knowing what we ate for breakfast? Or that we would become obsessed with watching cat videos on YouTube?

Likely not.

However, for nearly 50 years now, have been inundated with various iterations of news 24 hours a day. Checking social media is now a daily—if not hourly—activity for large swaths of our global population. And as our worlds become increasingly digital, an increasing volume of news and information is coming at us through a variety of online channels and voices.[122]

The changing news landscape and the advent of the Internet and digital, social, and mobile technologies have been some of the most profound disruptors to our communication environment of the last 50 years.

Our modern media and communication environment did not emerge out of nowhere though. It did not just pop up overnight. Rather, our current communication environment is a result of a set of changes in the way we communicate that has happened over the last several decades. So, how did this all come about?

The Changing News Landscape

News has always been a mix of serious and entertaining information. Stories of crime and politics have often been intermingled with stories about waterskiing squirrels or cats getting stuck in trees.[123]

This is nothing new.

However, it was really in the 1970s and 80s when we began to see the increasing erosion of this barrier between hard-hitting journalism and entertainment news when, amongst other things, the Cable News Network (CNN) launched. The brainchild of businessman, Ted Turner, CNN challenged the well-ingrained idea that news should be reported at a certain day and time and through select media voices.

While CNN aimed to highlight critical news stories from across the globe—like the Iran-Contra hearings and live coverage of the massacre at Tiananmen Square—it has really ended up being a media channel comprised of short political reports mixed with weather updates and human interest stories.[124]

Alongside CNN, all sorts of other types of "news" shows began to appear. For instance, we saw the idea of "reality news" emerge around this same time, which gave rise to "tabloid" news shows like *Inside Edition* and *Hard Copy*. These had the "look and feel" of news and were widely popular (ranking among the top 10 most popular shows at the time with millions of viewers) but really contained little substance.[125,126]

These changes to the news landscape resulted in substantial shifts in the kinds of information that people were exposed to and how such information was shared. These were the first signals that our media and communication environment was becoming increasingly fragmented, ubiquitous, and "always on." And it furthered this idea of "news as entertainment."

The Advent of the Internet and the Evolution of Digital, Social, and Mobile Technologies

While the changing news landscape substantially contributed to the fragmentation of our media and communication environment, it has really been the advent of the Internet—and the subsequent evolution of digital, social, and mobile technologies that have emerged because of it—that has given rise to some of the greatest and most recent changes to this environment.

And for better or worse, we have never been quite the same because of it.

Originally called ARPANET (Advanced Research Projects Agency Network), the Internet first originated in the 1960s when it was created as a way for government researchers to share information with one another.[127]

Since then—in the more than 50 years it has been around—the Internet has undergone substantial changes. As computer technology and programming power have evolved and improved, the "digital age" has unfolded before our eyes. This has made access easier and more ubiquitous—and increasingly the Internet has become ingrained in people's everyday lives. Today, more than 50% of the world's population[128] and more than 90% of American adults use the Internet.[129]

Further, it has brought with it an *endless* number of new technologies and innovations in media that have changed the way we communicate, interact, and navigate the world. These have included a wide variety of types of content, information, platforms, and formats.[130]

Perhaps more than we could have ever imagined were possible. Specifically, we have seen the emergence of:

- Online news;
- Literary and reference websites;
- eReaders (like the Kindle);
- Digital radio stations;
- Podcasts;
- Audiobooks;
- User-generated content;
- Streaming movie and television services;
- Virtual reality and simulations (such as Oculus Rift and Google Earth);
- Gaming platforms and mobile applications, or apps (such as Wordle, role-playing games (RPG), and Twitch).

We have also seen the emergence of social media and mobile devices during this time. It is estimated that more than 4.5 billion people worldwide currently use social media. That is more than double the estimated 2 billion social media users that existed just seven years ago.[131] As more and more people participate in social media, more and more of them have a platform on which—and an audience to which—to share their thoughts, opinions, and beliefs.[132]

Thus, the number and types of voices that disseminate all of this content have also changed. The advent of what we now call "social media influencers"—or everyday people who are incredibly influential within their online social networks[133]—has vastly shifted our digital ecosystem.

What makes this world of social media influencers so powerful is the fact that these online opinion leaders have large followings, who drive high engagement with their content, which, in turn, drives increased visibility of that content.[134] They, therefore, have the ability to help promote information that otherwise would not be seen.[135]

For better or for worse.

As well, the emergence of mobile devices, such as cell phones, smartphones, and iPads, has fueled access to digital information and use of social media even further. It is estimated that there are 7.1 billion mobile device users worldwide[136] and a whopping 85% of them access social media through their mobile devices.[137] This has made it possible for almost any person, anywhere, at any time to be connected to information while "on the go."[138,139]

As a result of this growth in digital and social media technologies, these have become pivotal communication tools for individuals, companies, organizations, and governments. The adoption of these tools for regular and everyday communication activities has resulted in the mushrooming of the volume and types of content created and shared in recent years.

To give you a sense of the size and scale of the amount of content that is now being created and shared through these digital tools, consider the following statistics. It is estimated that, as of 2019, more than 41.6 million mobile messages and 2.1 million "snaps" (on Snapchat) have been shared by online users globally.[140] As of 2020, it is estimated that over 500 hours of content are uploaded to the Internet every minute.[141] Finally, by 2025, it is estimated that there will be 175 *zettabytes* of data in the world. That is up from the approximate 2.5 *quintillion bytes* of data that we currently create every day.[142]

I do not even really know what a "zettabyte" is. I cannot even really describe how big that is, but I know it is big. Which means a lot of content is out there, available for people to consume, comprehend, and believe.

For better or for worse.

Mis- and Disinformation and Our Current Communication Environment

It is clear that our communication environment has undergone substantial change over the past 50 years, and these developments have resulted in many positive inventions and outcomes.

More people have access to information than ever before—and from almost anywhere.

The ability to create and share content with others is easier than ever before.

Mobile devices help leapfrog challenges with local internet service providers and put information at our fingertips.

Unfortunately, though, it is not all good news.

The vast amount of news and information that has been made available to us in recent years has increased the need to compete for eyeballs. This has led to sharing information in more compelling ways—by using graphical and video formats, more attention-grabbing headlines, and leveraging new and powerful voices—to stand out, gain attention, and drive views, shares, and clicks.

Naturally, the use of these tactics does not always mean that the best, highest quality, and most accurate information is being shared. No, it is usually the more sensational content that is shared. In fact, it is well documented how false or inaccurate information spreads more widely and quickly on social media—regardless of topic.[143]

This means that rumors and questionable information are more often amplified (compared to accurate information), which leads to the swift circulation of what we now refer to as "mis- or disinformation." This kind of information can be persuasive to people. And it is dangerous.

The rapid and broad dissemination of such information via these online sites and mobile apps is creating challenges with and barriers to the acceptance of critical evidence-based health-related information. Which is having life and death consequences. As Dr. Vivek H. Murthy, the U.S. Surgeon General, says,

> *Health misinformation is a serious threat to public health. It can cause confusion, sow mistrust, harm people's health, and undermine public health efforts. Limiting the spread of health misinformation is a moral and civic imperative that will require a whole-of-society effort.*[144]

We have seen this firsthand over the course of the COVID pandemic, as mis- and disinformation have impacted our ability to respond to the virus, message to people about risk and mitigation measures, curb the pandemic's impact, and save lives.

There are multiple reasons why we are seeing such a proliferation of this kind of false and inaccurate information occur. These are partly a factor of technology, but they are also a factor of how we process information. We discuss each of these next.

Information Processing and the Role of Cognitive Bias in Misinformation Dissemination

Why and how misinformation happens is, in part, due to how we process information. There is a lot of information available to us today, and our brains are just not built to process 175 zettabytes of content quickly or easily.

Unable to process all this information, we use shortcuts to help us. These shortcuts, or heuristics, help us decide what we should pay attention to and what we feel we can safely ignore. For instance ...

- We tend to remember things that fit well with what we already know and understand;
- We tend to pay closer attention to information from people we know and trust;
- We are more likely to share information with those we know and trust. [145]

Unfortunately, these mental "rules of thumb" can also result in irrational or inaccurate conclusions, or cognitive biases. Cognitive biases are errors in processing and interpreting information that result in our misunderstanding or misinterpreting patterns in the world. In doing so, we create new "subjective realities" that are based on inaccurate or incomplete information *(remember, context matters)*.[146] This, then, influences our judgments and behaviors. So we ...

- Tend to share narratives we like and that make sense to us;
- Join groups and communities that share our same beliefs, customs, and opinions;
- Resist information that does not conform to our beliefs or does not fit with our worldviews.

This can lead to bad decision-making based on bad information—and we are all guilty of it.

The Role of Digital Algorithms in Mis- and Disinformation Dissemination

So, there is a psychological aspect to why this proliferation of misinformation is happening—we just cannot handle all the information that is out there and available to us and we use tools to help us make sense of it all.

However, there is also an operational aspect to why this is occurring. While we are struggling to make sense of all the information that is available to us, digital technologies are taking advantage of our information processing shortcomings and giving us more of what we like and less of what we do not. Which is compounding the issue.

Particularly in digital and social media, it is happening because of how the algorithms that these sites employ operate. In short, they are built to amplify content with the highest engagement, the thinking around which goes something like …

> *Well, if it's getting a lot of engagement, of course it has to be a quality piece of content that others would also like to see.*

This makes sense—people want to see and engage with content that others seem to also like. And this is not new. We do this with the movies and television we watch and the music we listen to. We do this with the cultural and communal hobbies and activities we choose to engage in. People's likes and dislikes drive the content that they seek out and the activities they choose to engage in.

Online, this is exacerbated, however.

Online, it is happening faster, more ubiquitously, and across all topics (so yes, it happens with entertainment content, for sure, but it also happens with health, political, and world event content, just to name a few). So …

- Search engines direct people to sites that receive the most clicks;
- Social media connect people with other like-minded people;
- Social media users join groups oriented around similar interests and hobbies;
- Mobile apps and websites recommend products and services that are similar to ones that you have used or purchased in the past;
- Social media show users content that is similar to content they already like;
- And social media influencers are followed by people with common interests and beliefs.

Additionally, think about the language that mis- and disinformation uses compared to scientific information—it is just more alluring, more provocative, and more sensational.[147,148] It has to be to get the algorithms to work in its favor.

Fake information is just more interesting than real information.

Finally, the emergence of bots—automated accounts that impersonate humans—only serves to propel this further. Bots are artificially driving the visibility of and engagement with certain types of information (most often inaccurate and false information) and making it seem like something is more popular than it really is.[149–153]

Taken together, this means that exciting, interesting, and sensational content tends to be seen and shared more often, because generally that is what people like to see, read, and engage with. And mis- and disinformation, by its very nature, is mostly comprised of exciting, interesting, and sensational types of content.

Remember bleach and Ivermectin?

Therefore, mis- and disinformation tends to see higher visibility due to more users clicking, commenting, liking, and sharing this kind of information more frequently than other information. As Sinan Aral of the Massachusetts Institute of Technology said,

> *Falsehood diffuses significantly farther, faster, deeper, and more broadly than the truth in all categories of information.*[154]

This particular type of content is rewarded for its high engagement ... which drives, then, higher engagement ... which, then, is further rewarded by being shown more. It is a self-reinforcing cycle driven by a combination of what information we like, what information we think we need, and how technology enables both of those things.

Conclusion

All of this, taken together, has resulted in making our media and communication environment increasingly complex, dynamic, and challenging.

It is saturated with content.

It is overwhelmed by voices.

It is being driven by eyeballs, clicks, and code.

As humans, we are just not savvy enough to be able to navigate all of it well all of the time.

This has made communicating in this pandemic difficult.

These changes and their impact on pandemic communication further affirm the "mantra" that is now emerging in this book: Context matters.

Yes, similar strategies and tactics have been used during the influenza pandemic of 1918, over the course of the HIV/AIDS pandemic, and during the H1N1 pandemic in the early 2000s, but the media and communication context has dramatically shifted.

Also yes, CERC draws from many important theories and approaches to provide strategic and operational support to public health professionals dealing with emergencies and crisis situations, but the context for responding has vastly changed.

Finally, the rise of inaccurate and unsubstantiated counter-information (mis- and disinformation) has created all new contexts in which such information is accessed and shared.

So while clear, consistent, and regular messaging communicated via a mix of trusted voices, billboards, and digital ads is fine, in the context of more channels, more voices, more emphasis on sensationalist news—combined with a lack of trust—these will inevitably struggle to take hold, be seen, be attended to, and have an impact.

There is just so much more now that public health messaging is competing against.

Unfortunately, however, while, yes, pandemic messaging in our current media and communication environment does have a lot to compete with, some of the communication approaches employed over the course of the COVID pandemic have not helped make the situation any better. A myriad of messages has been shared over the course of the past several years—some of which have made sense, while others have appeared inconsistent and contradictory.

Understanding all the messaging we have been exposed to during this pandemic is worth some discussion, because we have been in this situation for over two years now and we have been told a lot of different things which have impacted our experiences in COVID. So next, we will look at the various phases of messaging that have occurred over the course of this pandemic, what we have been told, and how those messages have changed over time.

Chapter 5

Phases of Messaging

This is evolving science. You are seeing sausages being made—in front of the world's eyes.

—Saad Omer

COVID will go away.
Stay at home.
Stay six feet apart from other people.
You can gather in small groups.
You can gather outside.
Everything is reopening!
No need for masks.
Do not wear a mask unless you are sick.
If you really want to wear a mask, use a non-medical one.
Cloth masks do not protect as well as N95 or KN95 masks.
Actually, it is better if everyone wears a mask when in public or around others.
You must wear a mask. Even if you are healthy.
A vaccine is right around the corner.
A vaccine will not be available for months.
One dose. Two doses.
Everyone is going to need a booster.
Only those with chronic illnesses need a booster.
Now everyone should get one.
The vaccine offers freedom from COVID.

DOI: 10.4324/9781003267522-5

The vaccine will help reduce the severity of COVID and hospitalization. This is the new normal.

COVID will become endemic.

Sigh ... Do you feel me?

We have been through a lot over the course of this pandemic, and we have received a lot of different, and sometimes confusing, messaging through it all.

Am I the only one who feels like she has whiplash? I am sure I am not alone. It has been so confusing at times.

What should we listen to?

Whom should we believe?

Who is trustworthy in this situation?

This is life living in a pandemic ...

One that has played out on the global stage with different countries and communities using different and inconsistent approaches to handling the virus. The response to which was initially led by a government that questioned science (at least in the U.S.). That was supported, at least in the U.S., by a public health infrastructure that has been woefully underfunded for years. In a country where there is already low public trust.[155] That has occurred in a media and communication environment that enables *opinions about the pandemic* to be shared as surely as it does *scientific facts.*

Of course, it is complicated.

How could it not be?

And while all of this context is important—and has indeed contributed to the messy and confusing messaging that we have seen over the past several years—it is also incredibly important to remember that this pandemic brought a completely new virus into our lives. One that we had not seen before. A virus that we did not fully understand—that we are still learning about—despite its familiar lineage.

A Little Bit about COVID and the Scientific Process

COVID-19 is caused by the SARS-CoV-2 virus, which is from a family of coronaviruses. We have seen these before: There was the SARS coronavirus (SARS-CoV), which emerged in November 2002 and which causes severe acute respiratory syndrome (SARS). There was also the MERS coronavirus (MERS-CoV), which appeared in 2012 and causes MERS.[156,157]

While COVID-19 is related to these other strains, the virus itself, SARS-CoV-2, was new to us when it first showed up at the end of 2019. Hence, why we initially called it *novel*.[158] And exactly because it was new, our knowledge about it has evolved over time.

As happens when any new kind of scientific knowledge is gained.

The process of obtaining new scientific knowledge always involves the same five-step process—observation, hypothesis development, testing, analysis, and reporting,[159,160] Which is exactly the process that has been employed throughout this current pandemic.

Scientists first *observed* the virus, its characteristics, and how it has changed over time. This initially happened, of course, in the real world, when the virus first appeared towards the end of 2019 as well as over the course of the last several years as the virus has mutated. And with each new observation, a new *hypothesis has been made* (how it transmits, how it infects, etc.).

Tests have been developed and run. Unfortunately, again here, some of those "first tests" were the real-life infections and deaths that happened when the virus first emerged. Subsequently, however, new and additional experiments have been conducted in labs in order to learn more about the virus and try and get ahead of it (through the development of vaccines, antiviral pills, and other therapeutic treatments, etc.).

Data from both real-world scenarios and lab experiments have been *analyzed* on a regular and recurring basis as new situations and information have presented themselves, and finally, findings have been *reported* through data releases, peer-reviewed publications, and news stories.

The challenge with the scientific method is that it takes time and pandemics move fast.

Further, in the case of the COVID pandemic, the virus got a head start, initially appearing and infecting people before we knew what we were dealing with.

Given all of this, the information, findings, and messages that scientists, public health professionals, health communicators, policy-makers, and others have shared over the course of the COVID pandemic have often quickly appeared out-of-date, irrelevant, inconsistent, or just plain wrong.

So, our perceptions and feelings that the messaging disseminated during this pandemic has been confusing are not necessarily wrong.

They are not necessarily right though either.

Exploring these messages, the phases of them, and how they have rolled out over the last several years is important to understand how pandemic messaging has shifted in our current context—in part as a result of the changing nature of the virus but also as a result of other policies, pressures, and politics that influenced said messaging.

This will be the focus of the rest of this chapter: Reviewing the various phases of the pandemic, as they happened, along with the messages that accompanied them.

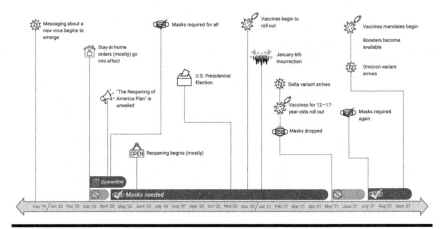

Figure 5.1 Phases of Messaging Timeline.

Amelia Burke-Garcia.

The following discussion is broken up into phases (pre-pandemic, quarantine, vaccine rollout, amongst others) and, as with the rest of this book, is based on a mix of my personal experiences, stories, and memories from over the course of the pandemic and findings from an assessment of news articles from across this time period. To orient you to the phases and events I review in the next section, Figure 5.1 presents a timeline that summarizes these phases and the key messages that were circulating during them.

Now, on to the good stuff.

Pre-pandemic Messaging about a New Virus

I remember the exact moment I heard about COVID for the very first time. It was early one morning in December of 2019 and I was sitting on the couch in my living room at home.

I remember that moment so clearly.

I recall reading the news on my phone that morning and there was a story about a virus in Wuhan, China that was infecting people. The story stated that the virus had not spread too far—and that it was not in the U.S. yet. At the time, I had no idea what that story would mean for us just a few months later, but I do recall thinking in that moment,

> *What do you mean, it is not in the U.S. yet? Of course, it is here.*
> *It is definitely already here.*

Even though I thought at the time that the virus *had* to be here, what I was not thinking about—what I could not have conceived of in that moment—was how it would, quite quickly, become such a big issue here in the U.S. and around the world.

How it would drastically change all of our lives.

My experiences and expectations at that time were likely largely driven by what was being said in the news (as we have just discussed, the news media can shape our perceptions of key issues)—and the common messages in the media during this time were that this was not a big deal.

At that time (late December 2019), the news of the emergence of a "mysterious pneumonia" in Wuhan, China was a relatively minor part of the news cycle. Initial statements in the news about COVID downplayed the threat of the disease, noted that there were no reported cases in the U.S., and highlighted that public health officials were assessing the threat of the virus as low. Instead, the news was largely dominated by the Democratic primary race and the teen vaping crisis *(do you even remember that?)*.

As we all know now, however, in just a few weeks' time, this would all change as the first case of the virus in the U.S. was reported in January 2020. This was also the first time the virus would be labeled "a coronavirus."[161-165]

Moving into Quarantine

As we rang in the new year and moved from the first reports of a faraway virus (in 2019) to the first reported cases in the U.S. (in 2020), nothing seemed to change much initially. At least, for me personally. I still went to work. I still traveled. I still went out to dinner with friends. Nothing was really modified or stopped in those early days.

Honestly, as I think back to that time, I think the things I worried about most in the winter of 2020 had to do with catching a cold from someone or getting stuck traveling somewhere due to inclement weather. COVID was not a worry. It was not even on my radar.

Then, March arrived, and things rapidly changed from there. Work places began telling people not to come into the office anymore. Restaurants and businesses began to shutter.

Some people started wearing masks.

We all started to go home. We all started to prepare for quarantine—but with no idea how long we would be in it.

Some people started stockpiling food. I remember so clearly being at the grocery store with my husband trying to figure out what to do. Most of the food was already gone from the shelves the day we went, and we were asking each other,

How much pasta do we really need?

How many cans of beans should we buy?

How many cans of beans *does* one need to feel secure in the beginning phases of a global pandemic? When you do not really know what you are scared about? Or how long it will last? Or when the next time you will go to the grocery store will be?

We had no idea.

I think we bought four cans of black beans and four cans of red kidney beans and four boxes of pasta.

We had no clue what was going on. What we were in for.

We were so ignorant in those early days. Naïve and unprepared.

And initial messaging during this phase highlighted these exact things. Prominent in the media's narratives were the topics of stay-at-home and quarantine orders. Most of the messaging followed the direction of the White House at the time, which was recommending a quarantine of no more than two weeks and touting the need for only a short period of stringent stay-at-home measures to stop the spread of the virus.

Messaging did vary widely at the local level though. Depending on where you lived and worked—and especially if you lived in one place and worked in another (like so many of us do in the U.S.)—the guidance could vary widely depending on which state you were in, or even what city or county you were in.

Other messaging at this time focused on the critical shortages of goods and supplies (paper products, hand sanitizer, soap, and other cleaning products). News of panic buying was everywhere as we all grappled with this new way of living.

Finally, masking guidance was also beginning to appear around this time but would be shared in as equally a disjointed manner as the quarantine orders. Based on early guidance from the WHO and CDC, some people had started to wear masks during this time but others were still reluctant to do so.

Regardless of some people's reluctance to wear masks, with panic buying setting in, masks were becoming scarce. So, following this, Americans were initially advised not to buy or wear masks with the understanding that they were not really necessary to protect oneself from COVID.

Later, however, this guidance would be further clarified to convey that while, yes, masks indeed work, the limited supply of vital personal protective equipment (PPE) needed to be preserved for medical professionals who were treating patients as well as others working on the front lines of the pandemic.

Even though the mask debate would end up dragging on for much of the pandemic (we will discuss this in more detail throughout the rest of this chapter), these early days saw the beginnings of what would become very mixed and confusing messaging about masks.

Taken together, all of this mixed messaging was beginning to cause substantial confusion and anxiety amongst people.[166–172]

In Quarantine and Stay-At-Home Measures

Then, we went home. For good.

No going out. No going to restaurants. No movies or live music.

We were all at home. Alone. Together.

And what a time that was.

Overall, during this time, things were fine for me. As I mentioned at the beginning of this book, my husband and I were lucky enough to both keep our jobs when the pandemic hit. We both have positions where we could continue to work remotely without much interruption. We also have the space to do so relatively comfortably.

I know this was—and is—not the case for everyone.

I know many others had a harder time.

People in small apartments, who live with multiple family members.

People who have children and who were all of a sudden having to coordinate both remote school and work.

People who could not work from home and therefore, had to go to work and risk infection (and risk the possibility of bringing the virus home).

People were having all sorts of different experiences during this time in quarantine. And the messaging from this time reflected many of these things: Adapting to stay-at-home orders, the attempts that businesses and schools were making to move operations to remote settings, and the catastrophic job loss that was throttling the U.S. economy as things shut down.

As well, some of the first messaging about the disparate economic impacts began to appear around this time as we started to see stark differences in how people were able to cope with the challenges of those early days. Some people (white collar workers) could stay home and stay safe from the virus, while others (most often women and members of racial and ethnic communities) had to continue to go to work, putting themselves at higher risk for infection and death.

And as people struggled to adjust to our new reality, reports of how it was impacting people's mental health also began to surface.

Finally, news reports about the tension between the states and the federal government to enforce stay-at-home orders also started circulating during this time. Many states were not adhering to federal recommendations, were slow to implement protective measures, and were trying to push for reopening to bring their economies back. All of this mixed messaging, disagreement, and lack of coordination just continued to fuel the confusion and unrest that was already being felt nationwide.[173–178]

To Wear a Mask or Not Wear a Mask

Oh, the mask debate.

This issue has been with us pretty much since the beginning of the pandemic and continues even as I write these pages. So, you know we *have* to cover this aspect of pandemic messaging.

As noted earlier, at the outset of the pandemic, the WHO and CDC were telling the public to wear masks if they were sick.[179] However, as news of the pandemic spread and panic buying increased, toilet paper was not the only thing to quickly fly off the shelves of stores. Masks were another one of those items that people began stocking up on. Specifically, people began stockpiling N95 masks.

Officially called "N95 Filtering Facepiece Respirators" (or N95 FFRs or N95 respirators, for short), an N95 respirator can filter out at least 95% of very small (0.3 micron) particles from the air, including bacteria and viruses, and are most commonly used in healthcare settings by personnel who need protection from both airborne and fluid hazards (e.g., splashes, sprays).[180]

The critical need for these special masks for frontline workers soon became clear. As hospitals became overwhelmed with COVID patients, these specific masks became necessary to protect these workers from the virus. But the panic buying had made them scarce.

So, in March 2020, in order to help curb the worldwide shortage of masks, the message about wearing a mask if sick shifted to a message about not needing to wear a mask.[181,182]

Then, the asymptomatic cases[183,184] began showing up. An asymptomatic case refers to:

A person infected with COVID who does not develop symptoms.[185]

And we soon realized that not only could someone have COVID and not have any symptoms, but that these asymptomatic cases could also still spread the virus, making masks incredibly important to slowing the spread of infection.

In July 2020, CDC released a Morbidity and Mortality Weekly Report (MMWR) about the benefits of mask-wearing. In light of all the asymptomatic cases that were occurring, masks were re-recommended.[186]

So, the guidance changed yet again.[187,188]

Following the release of this MMWR, in September 2020, then-CDC Director, Dr. Robert Redfield, came out publicly in support of mask-wearing, saying that the wearing of a mask is the most powerful tool the nation has to curb the spread of the virus.[189]

So you would think, after all of that, it would be settled.

There was new evidence *and* an MMWR to support the role of masks in reducing the risk of COVID transmission. You would think that the messaging on this topic would be clear and would be universally accepted and followed.

But as we all know now, it would not turn out this way. It would not be that easy.

In response to Dr. Redfield's comment about mask-wearing, then-President Trump pushed back. He rebuked the usefulness of masks, and in doing so, set off further confusion and discord.[190] Despite this in-fighting, health authorities went on to continue to advise mask-wearing throughout the 2020–2021 winter season as cases continued to rise.

As you may expect, the messaging from across this time period reflected these topics and controversies. It mostly focused on the back-and-forth about mask-wearing, with some commentaries highlighting mask-wearing as "a public health imperative" while others described mask mandates as "coercive government control."

Additionally, this period of time saw coverage of the other disagreements that were occurring between government and public health leaders about other COVID response protocols (e.g., social distancing protocols, reopening, the timing of the availability of a vaccine, etc.).

We also saw during this time the various political movements and demonstrations begin to emerge in reaction to and retaliation against government and public health officials' COVID-related guidelines. And the media highlighted these, emphasizing how such discord amongst the nation's top leaders and experts only served to cause greater confusion among the general population.[191–196]

Phased Reopening

As the month of March wore on and we had no idea how long quarantine would last, people started to become antsy.

Businesses were losing money.

Shops were closing.

People were out of work.

People were getting angry.

Politicians were getting scared.

How were they going to balance managing the public health crisis that was COVID *and* keep their economies running?

It was around April 2020 when the Trump Administration started to unveil their ideas about whether and how states could begin to ease stay-at-home measures, begin to reopen businesses, and allow people to get back to their normal activities.

Ultimately, they left the decision-making about reopening up to the states but laid out several guidelines to help states make these decisions:

- There had to have been a downward trajectory in influenza-like illnesses in a state for 14 days;
- There had to have been a downward trajectory in COVID cases in a state for 14 days;
- Testing programs, including antibody testing, had to have been set up for at-risk healthcare workers;
- And healthcare providers in a state had to have the capacity to treat all COVID patients without operating under a crisis care plan.

The plan was called, "The Reopening of America"[197] and with this guidance, states began assessing their ability to reopen.

However, this plan meant that every state, county, and city was putting in place different approaches to and rules about reopening based on their individual assessments of the White House's guidance. This meant that for individuals, the process—what was allowed and what was required—continued to be confusing, varied, and mostly unclear.

Thus, we saw during this time more confusing processes, with more confusing messaging, yet again. These messages focused on revitalizing the American economy and getting people back to business. News coverage highlighted the decimation of the small business industry and emphasized the need to reopen to protect against economic catastrophe. Figuring out how to do this—to manage the severe economic downturn in the country despite a pandemic that continued to rage—was a struggle and continued to be a focus for everyone.

Finally, as businesses began to reopen, messaging shifted to highlight the plight of schools, where the fate of reopening in-person still remained a big question.[198–202]

Keep in mind that this was still only April of 2020. This was all happening *just weeks* after the initial outbreak in the U.S. and the quarantine orders. *Just weeks!* We know now that the pandemic was far from being over at this time and that there was still so much more that would come.

The Vaccine Roll Out

Up until this point in the pandemic, there had been some messaging about a new vaccine, but a lot remained unclear and unconfirmed. While the vaccine was being touted as offering us "freedom from COVID," questions remained regarding the speed of development, timing of federal approval, and the country's ability to conduct a nationwide roll out.

It was on this topic where, yet again, Dr. Redfield would face another dispute with then-President Trump. At that same press conference in September 2020, where he spoke about the importance of mask-wearing, Dr. Redfield said that a COVID vaccine would likely not be widely available to the general public until the spring or summer of 2021. Trump responded to this, just hours later, rebuking Dr. Redfield and saying, instead, that distribution could come as early as October or November 2020, with as many as 100 million doses available by the end of 2020.

We were seeing all of this messaging and counter messaging and there wasn't even a vaccine yet.

Despite this apparent in-fighting within the Trump Administration, the vaccine was truly viewed during this time as the best way to end the pandemic. The vaccine was our singular hope—and was touted as such—and this message would continue to circulate well beyond this period of time.

Past the 2020 Election.

Past the January 6th Insurrection.

Past the swearing-in of the new President of the United States, Joe Biden, in 2021.

All the way into the summer of 2021.

And with that message, it finally happened. The first vaccines began to roll out.

I remember that time so acutely. I was so excited to get my first dose of the vaccine. I could not wait. It was the first time since the pandemic started and we went into stay-at-home measures that I felt a true glimmer of hope. I remember getting my first shot and just feeling so optimistic for the future. It was only the first shot—and I knew that I needed several weeks and another dose to be considered full vaccinated—and yet, hope was the only thing I felt that day.

The rollout began in December 2020, prioritizing certain audiences first. Older adults. People living with pre-existing health conditions. Those working on the frontlines or with vulnerable communities. Then, as the new year rolled around, the vaccines would start to become more widely available. With this, a whole new round of messaging—and fighting—began.[203]

Overall, at this time, the news broadly promoted the availability of the vaccine with much praise for the efforts to develop one so quickly. Additionally, many people were eager to get vaccinated in those early days.

Yet, after the initial wave of vaccines rolled out, vaccination rates started to stagnate. In particular, African American/Black and Hispanic/Latino communities were expressing heightened apprehension and perceived distrust of the vaccine, as were many from both the political and ideological left and right. Some people questioned how a vaccine could come to market so quickly. Others questioned its safety and efficacy.

Suddenly, with that, the idea of a future "free from COVID" was thrown into jeopardy.

The messaging that was circulating at this point highlighted this hesitancy and the stagnation of the roll out. Our ability to combat the pandemic with a vaccine came into question. And with so many vaccines going unused in the U.S. due to this hesitancy, some messages critiqued the country for not donating more doses to other countries that needed—*and wanted*—them.

With vaccine hesitancy circulating and the rollout slowing down, new methods to encourage and require vaccination started to emerge. It was in September of 2021 when some of the first discussions of vaccine mandates for certain types of businesses, locations, and job types started to appear.

Not surprisingly, this also caused great divisions amongst people. Subsequently, the messaging changed from highlighting the benefits of the vaccine to highlighting the divisions between people, businesses, politicians, and governing bodies, due to the debate about mandates. The news media at the time featured these things prominently: The anger from people and businesses, the dissention from city and county leaders, the public pushback from other politicians, the need to provide proof of vaccination, and the related fights that were beginning to take place in courtrooms across the country.

As we look back at this time, the coverage of the vaccine differed depending on where we were in the process and who was speaking. As with so many other COVID-related topics, the messaging of this time was disjointed, unclear, and confusing. As such, it did not always lend itself well to addressing people's questions or concerns; rather, it continued to be a catalyst for conflict.[204–208]

To Wear a Mask or Not Wear a Mask—Redux

Mask-wearing has been one of the more controversial, confusing, mis-messaged, politicized, and polarizing topics of the pandemic. And as we now know, the debate that started in early 2020 was far from over.

As we headed into the summer of 2021, and the vaccine roll out was fully underway, initial vaccination rates looked promising and the case burden of COVID was beginning to diminish.

Yet, as we just discussed, despite these advances, the overall vaccination trend had begun to slow down. To encourage more people to get vaccinated, CDC released guidance in May 2021 that said that fully vaccinated people did not have to wear masks anymore—indoors and out.[209]

This was, in part, due to what was known about the science at the time. It was thought that if you were vaccinated, you could not spread COVID to someone else, making the mask unnecessary. As well, the dangerous Delta variant was starting to circulate (and would eventually become the dominant variant) so public health leaders were motivated to get as many people vaccinated as quickly as possible during this time—and saw the ability to safely drop the mask if vaccinated as an incentive to do so.

This made the message that "you could safely drop the mask if you were vaccinated" sound from both an epidemiological standpoint as well as a public relation's one. Or so we thought.

Unfortunately, as we now know, new evidence emerged that suggested that vaccinated people could still spread COVID. Thus, the mask debate did another about-face in just a matter of months. Just as quickly as we were told we could drop the mask if vaccinated, we were told to put the mask back on.

News coverage at this time highlighted this ping-ponging messaging. Figure 5.2 shows the quickly shifting media coverage of the mask-wearing guidance—just three months apart. The image on the left shows a news report from May 2021 about the guidance that masks are not required for fully vaccinated people, while the image on the right shows a news report from July 2021 about the reversal of the mask-wearing guidance.

This was commonly perceived as the government and public health experts "moving the goalpost" for this pandemic. It added to the existing perception and belief that the approach to dealing with this pandemic was inconsistent and confusing. And provided little comfort that we were getting closer to ending it. It also caused further conflict and division.

Delta, Omicron, and Boosters, Oh My!

Following the stumbles that occurred during the roll out of the vaccine and the second wave of mask-wearing debates, the hits just kept on coming. During this time, we saw the emergence of new variants, the approval of vaccines for kids ages 12–17 years old, and the availability of booster shots.

The messaging of the time reflected these topics and people's sentiments about them. The Delta variant arrived in the summer of 2021 and further complicated the progress being made regarding vaccination, as cases surged, and

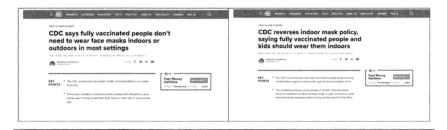

Figure 5.2 Side-by-Side Media Headlines Show Mask-Wearing Guidance About-Face.[210,211]

CNBC.

the effectiveness of the vaccine in preventing infection came under additional scrutiny. Delta also caused renewed concerns around the pandemic's longevity and whether we would ever be able to get out of this situation.

Amidst Delta, vaccines for 12–17-year-olds were approved, and parents and families had to start to make the decision to vaccinate their kids or not. This raised all sorts of questions and discussions for parents about vaccinating their children and the safety of the COVID vaccine.[212]

Complicating this was the emergence of select cases of myocarditis (heart inflammation) in kids after getting vaccinated. After investigating these cases, CDC determined that the rate of occurrence was low and that cases tended to be mild, and confirmed that it was still safe for children to get the vaccine.[213]

However, the news coverage of these cases further fueled the mis- and disinformation about the vaccine as well as the anti-vaccination campaigns that were ramping up during this time. These anti-vaccination messages would continue to circulate broadly and widely into the 2021–2022 winter season, with some purporting that COVID itself poses less risk to children than the vaccine.[214] As a result, the vaccination rates of minors in the U.S. began to slow, somewhat mirroring what was being seen in the adult population during this time.

Delta began to wane in the fall of 2021 but then, just as quickly, the Omicron variant began to emerge, raging across the U.S. and around the globe and creating new surges in the number of cases and deaths.

With Omicron, the world was confronted with the sobering reality that the pandemic would likely not have a definitive "end point."

Does that sound familiar to you? 'Cuz that is exactly how I felt during this time.

I have described Omicron as the real "gut punch" of the pandemic *for me*. It was particularly hard, I think, because I had been truly excited to get vaccinated against COVID, and as things seemed to start to get better and began to reopen, my husband and I started to venture back out into the world and do some of the things that we always loved to do but had not done regularly since before the pandemic started.

Yet, just as we started to do those things again—see friends, see family, travel on planes, go out to restaurants—so many people we knew got sick. So we put that all back on hold.

And that was the "gut punch."

It was one thing to give things up during the early days of the pandemic. It was not necessarily easy but it was necessary. And we were fine with it. You learn to live differently. Do different things. Engage in different activities.

However, to begin to return to your old activities and your old way of living, doing the things you love but had not been able to do for a couple of years—and then to have all of that taken away *again* ... yeah, that was hard for me.

But so it went. For me and for all of us.

Omicron swiftly became the dominant strain in the U.S. yet vaccination rates remained stagnant. With that, many officials appeared to be at a loss as to how to increase vaccination rates without further mandates. It was largely discussed during this time—and broadly accepted by many—that lockdowns would be an unacceptable measure for dealing with the surges of these new variants.

Further, while public health officials in many jurisdictions did revert back to requiring masks and social distancing as mitigation strategies, others remained reluctant to put any of these pre-vaccine requirements back in place. Thus, the disjointed nature of our pandemic response and use of mitigation strategies continued.

Then, booster shots arrived. Initially recommended for high-risk adults, these were later approved for all adults. As the Omicron variant raged on, messaging around the importance of boosters became more common in the news media, as authorities tried to encourage people to get a booster to strengthen their immunity.

Despite this, additional questions began to circulate during this time around vaccine effectiveness as data demonstrated decreased effectiveness of the vaccine over time and against these new variants. Rumors also began circulating about the changing definition of "fully vaccinated" and the possible inclusion of booster shots in that definition.

As a result, we saw the increasing use of new messaging related to the vaccine's effectiveness—but these new messages highlighted the vaccine's ability to reduce the severity of infection and the risk of hospitalization and death from COVID. With that, the mantra—"freedom from COVID"—that we had previously heard touted widely over the course of the pandemic slowly started to fade.

With this change in messaging came the deeper understanding that the pandemic was not over and that there really was no end in sight. As such, our hope for the eradication of the virus began to dwindle. Eventually, we would start to see messaging about COVID becoming "endemic." Or always with us *(remember Chapter 2?)*.

With that, people's mental health and emotional well-being became further strained as the pandemic continued to drag on. As we headed into 2022 and approached the third year of the pandemic with no real end in sight *(can you believe I just wrote those words!)*, messaging shifted to focus on the will of the people to manage through this ongoing pandemic and to comply with continued COVID restrictions and mandates.

Divisions between people, families, communities, and political parties also increased, and the economy continued to struggle with inflation during this time.

Naturally, news coverage continued to highlight these things: The length of the pandemic, the increasing number of cases due to Omicron, the conflict and divisions, and the economic impact.[215–221] These twists and turns with the new variants, the need for boosting, and the unending life of the pandemic just served to further exacerbate the perceived "moving goalpost" philosophy and continued to complicate public health guidance and messaging, as the context and needs continued to change.

Again. And again. And again.

Conclusion

Ooh boy. That was depressing.

I know. All that we have gone through. All that we have had to deal with.

It *is* depressing.

However, this review of the pandemic phases, and the messages that dominated each, is really meant to demonstrate how different topics were in-focus at different times and how the messaging that characterized these phases reflected an environment that was shifting quickly and often.

It also really calls out to us—pointedly—how messaging throughout this pandemic has been complicated, unclear, politically charged, and seemingly controversial as a result. This, in turn, has caused increasing confusion and distrust amongst people.

It has not been easy. For any of us.

And yet, while we have all gone through these same phases and been inundated with the same kinds of messages, the fact is, we have not all experienced the pandemic in the same way. I have already shared with you some of my own experiences over the course of this pandemic. Now we need to look at the experiences of others. This shall be the focus of our next chapter.

Chapter 6

Audience Group Experiences

We don't see things as they are, we see them as we are

—Anaïs Nin

We have been saying, throughout the first several chapters of this book, how not everyone has experienced COVID in exactly the same way. To talk about differing experiences in the COVID pandemic, however, is not just to talk about how the Netflix show I binged-watched was different from the Netflix show you binged-watched. Rather, there have been disparities in experiences related to people's health, safety, well-being, and ability to thrive. Experiences related to...

The risk of infection.
Quarantine and shutdowns.
The need to work.
Food and housing insecurity.
Dwelling type.
Geographic location.
Distrust. Mistrust.
Being a parent.
Being a caretaker.
Accessing health care.
The digital divide.
Access to telehealth.

DOI: 10.4324/9781003267522-6

Risk of death.

Digital literacy.

Misinformation.

Disinformation.

Despite the universality of COVID, experiences with it have differed for many individuals and communities. Here in the U.S. as well as around the world. Which have made each of our situations unique.

Context has mattered.

Moreover, these different pandemic experiences reveal deeper, more substantial disparities in terms of people's lived experiences more generally—with or without a pandemic. This makes exploring these experiences from a variety of perspectives both interesting and worthwhile.

In 2020, the New York Times ran an article that did just that: It featured the stories of several people in the U.S. and what their experiences had been like in COVID.[222] The stories they featured exemplify the varied experiences in COVID specifically, but they also help to illustrate those deeper, more substantial realities that people have been living with long before COVID.

It highlighted just how different these can be.

To begin our conversation about different communities' experiences in COVID, I wanted to share these stories with you.

Meet Issouf Mande

Mr. Mande moved to New Jersey from Burkina Faso in 2017 and got a job delivering pizza for Domino's. At the time of this story, he had had this job for about two years.

When COVID hit, some restaurants closed completely but others remained open, offering take out and delivery as ways to continue to make money. Domino's was one of those companies.

With people dining out less, takeout and food delivery options became the predominant options for ordering food in the pandemic—and the businesses that remained open and offered these options reaped the benefits.[223,224] For instance, food delivery service app companies such as GrubHub, DoorDash, Uber Eats, and Postmates reportedly earned more than twice as much in revenue during the pandemic compared to the year prior.[225]

However, while businesses have been able to stay afloat because of delivery options, it's the people—like Mr. Mande—who have been on the frontlines and providing these essential services who have felt the real impact. They are the ones doing the actual deliveries and who have gone out, knocked on doors, and brought people their food. They are the ones who have been continually exposed to the virus because of their jobs. They are the ones who have taken all the risks.

As Mr. Mande said,

> *I am scared of the virus because I'm going everywhere, opening every kind of door, going to any kind of house, meeting any kind of people. I think it's not safe. We meet so many people in deliveries. I don't see enough protection.*

Meet Darlyne Dagrin

Ms. Dagrin is a working mother with a young son. At the time of this story, her son was 22 months old and she was working full-time at a nursing home in Cedar Grove, New Jersey. Before the pandemic, she would drop her son off at a daycare facility on her way to work. When the pandemic hit, though, the daycare center had to close temporarily. But Ms. Dagrin's nursing home did not close during the pandemic so she still had to go to work.

This left her with few options for childcare. She would often try and find a friend or a relative to care for her son while she was at work, but if she could not find someone, she had to miss work.

That meant that she did not get paid on those days. Her job was also threatened because she had to miss work so often. Those were her choices. Take care of her child or earn a living. She said,

> *This week I called out twice. They called me and said: We won't accept no more callouts. If you call out again you're out of a job.*

Meet Maggie Russell-Ciardi

Ms. Russell-Ciardi is a working mom of a three-year-old son (at the time of this story). She works as a nonprofit consultant in New York City and as a part-time yoga teacher.

Despite having a similar situation to Mr. Mande (her job as a yoga instructor means that she interacts with people face-to-face) and to Ms. Dagrin (being a working mother), Ms. Russell-Ciardi's experience in COVID has been vastly different from theirs.

While the pandemic certainly changed things for Ms. Russell-Ciardi, her particular circumstances meant that she could more comfortably adjust to the changes the pandemic was precipitating. Being a nonprofit consultant, she was able to maintain her job and transition her work to a remote environment. Therefore, she was able to keep her son at home with her. Additionally, as she worked as a consultant, she had the flexibility to schedule her work around her son's sleep and play schedules. She also was able to continue to teach yoga, as virtual classes became a regular thing for yoga studios in the pandemic.

These adjustments did require that she work odd hours sometimes, like waking up early to get something done while her son still slept. It also meant that things did not always go as planned, and she would have to make do if her son woke up early from a nap or did not sleep when she thought he would. She said,

> *It's better for me to do my own practice when he's sleeping. But it's nice to have him growing up feeling like he's part of the yoga community even if it's now a virtual one. It's an important teaching for him.*

The pandemic has necessitated the making of impossible choices—take care of a loved one or take care of a job; put food on the table and pay bills or risk getting sick. It has also accentuated people's delicate economic situations in this country—and around the globe. Finally, it has underscored the lack of options for caretaking (whether for a child or other family member) in this country.

Mr. Mande and Ms. Dagrin's stories showcase these issues and how the pandemic has exacerbated them. They have had to make choices. In doing so, they have been forced to prioritize either their health and their family's well-being or their ability to take care of their basic needs.

Ms. Russell-Ciardi, on the other hand, *never* had to choose between earning a living and paying bills, taking care of her child, and the risk of getting sick. She could easily keep working, take care of her child, and keep her risk of infection from COVID lower. She was able to adjust her work and personal life in ways that Mr. Mande and Ms. Dagrin could not.

These are real people, and these are their real stories. About choice. About prioritization. And not all stories are the same.

I do not mean to suggest that the stress that families have had to endure with simultaneous remote school, childcare, and work has not been real or hard, but it is important to note that there is a fundamental difference between the experiences of people and families who have had the opportunity for all of that compared to the experiences of those who have not. To be forced to choose between health and security is a terrible choice to have to make, and it has had a profound effect on people over the course of this pandemic.

Exploring these differences is critical as we think about the course of this pandemic, what we have experienced, how we have been impacted, how those experiences have been unique, and how all of this ties into pandemic communication. Below, I explore some of what is in the literature and media about different audiences' experiences amid COVID, with a particular focus on communities that have traditionally been un- or underrepresented and forgotten about.

Different Community Experiences in COVID

Over the course of this book, we have talked about the importance of acknowledging how different people have had different experiences in COVID. How context matters.

Thus far, though, we have just scratched the surface of this topic. In fact, there is a lot more to talk about related to it. Below, we discuss in greater detail the different experiences that various communities have had in this pandemic. We will cover a wide variety of groups such as older adults, caregivers, teachers, children and youth, the LGBTQIA (lesbian, gay, bisexual, transgender, queer, questioning, intersex, asexual, and agender) community, essential workers, healthcare workers, and people experiencing homelessness, among others. Some have endured really tough experiences while others have gone through a range of them. We will discuss each, in turn, but we will begin with older adults.

Older Adults

Certainly, older adults (which I am defining here as people ages 65 and older) have experienced their fair share of varying experiences in COVID. During this time, primary concerns amongst this group have been worry and stress about the virus and infection. They have been the group most likely to see the pandemic as a major threat to their physical health.[226]

Additionally, reports of loneliness have been common. This is due, in large part, to the required mitigation measures that we all have had to take to slow the spread of the virus and reduce the risk of infection (things such as quarantining, limitations on activities, and social distancing). These things have all had negative impacts on older adults.

In particular, older adults within the LGBTQIA community have suffered from social isolation in COVID. While this had been a chronic issue before COVID, the pandemic has only served to exacerbate these feelings of loneliness.[227]

However, it has not been *all bad* for the older adult group. In fact, their experiences overall have been mixed, and some have actually thrived during this time.[228]

Generally speaking, many of them have seen the pandemic as less of a threat to their personal financial situations, and many have reported experiencing joy and comfort as a result of their relationships, the ability to digitally connect, and their hobbies.[229]

This ability to cope and be resilient through this time may stem from the fact that this group, by definition, is, well, *older*. They, therefore, have a wider range of life experiences upon which to draw when confronted with tough times. A larger "resiliency" toolbox, so to speak. This gives them specific coping skills that may have helped them view the pandemic in a different light than maybe some other communities.

Caregivers

Caregivers is another group that has also had a range of experiences.[230]

Caregiving is a challenging role to play in the best of circumstances. It is a lot of responsibility to care for someone else, be it a child, parent, friend, or relative who requires ongoing attention and support (due to medical, physical, social, emotional, or psychological needs). Balancing the act of caregiving AND taking care of all the other responsibilities we have—like work, health, and finances—can be overwhelming.

Add to this all the challenges of COVID. COVID has caused concerns about infection for people who are already at risk. It has caused disruptions in services for those who need regular care (medical or otherwise). It has created new family dynamics, as family members had to learn to come together to support one another or stay apart to avoid infection. It also has created rifts in families and communities as opinions differed about how to stay safe, slow or stop the spread of the virus, and protect those being cared for.

Ultimately, COVID has manifested *additional* stressors for a group that was already dealing with a lot of stress. And we can see how people's caregiving struggles have been amplified. *(Remember, Ms. Dagrin?)*

While caregivers have struggled, though, there have been some bright spots. They have been able to adapt and find new ways to be caregivers in the pandemic. They have leveraged technology to help with appointments, connections, and ordering needed services and products. They have also created new routines to adapt to the disruptions that COVID has caused, create some flexibility in their schedules, and get things done as they need to be done.[231]

Parents and Families

One of the groups hardest hit by the pandemic has been families and, in particular, parents.

A type of "caregiver," the pandemic has disrupted traditional routines and rules for families. In COVID, schedules and rituals for school, homework, hobbies, and meals have shifted, requiring families to come up with new ways of doing things in order to adapt to this new environment.[232,233]

They have worn many hats and played many roles amid this pandemic. Parents have had to care for their kids during COVID, manage remote school, re-envision hobbies (since many activities ceased altogether or were moved online and held virtually), all the while handling their own work responsibilities (remote or in-person) and other home responsibilities at the same time.

One study from Australia found that, in the pandemic, the time parents spent doing paid work was actually less than the time spent doing unpaid work (i.e., housework, childcare). Fathers in this study, in particular, reported doing more than their normal share of housework and childcare in quarantine and reported greater dissatisfaction with their work–family balance.[234]

During this time, many parents have also lost their access to support systems, whether due to illness or death from COVID, social distancing from family and friends, or the closure of childcare services. We saw this in the story about Ms. Dagrin earlier in this chapter. This has been the case for *both* single and dual-earner households.

Some parents have also had to take on *new* caregiving roles in the pandemic. Some already lived with extended family and needed to step up to help them more during this time. Others have had friends or family move in with them during the pandemic. Either way, these additional roles have been a cause of great stress and worry for parents and families.

Finally, financial difficulties have also been a substantial cause of stress for this group. Many parents have worried about paying for housing, food, and other bills due to under- or unemployment in the pandemic.[235] Then, for parents who had to work, but who could not do their jobs remotely, the risk of exposure to the virus, getting sick, and possibly bringing it back to their families caused additional anxiety.

Overall, this group has been stressed. COVID has created a perfect storm wherein parental roles and responsibilities have needed to increase, but simultaneously, access to supports and resources has decreased, exacerbating an already stressful situation.

Schools, Teachers, and Students

Schools, teachers, and students have also struggled tremendously during the course of the pandemic.

Whether we're talking about the beginning of the pandemic when COVID forced schools to close and teachers had to conduct their classes remotely,[236–239] or later in the pandemic as schools had to decide if and how to reopen, how to organize classrooms in a socially distancing world, how to quarantine students who got sick, and what to do about mask-wearing[240–244]—the impact has been profound.

The pandemic has greatly disrupted the teaching and learning process. Teachers have not always had adequate resources with which to do their jobs successfully or access to the right technologies with which to teach lesson plans remotely. These things created challenges for teachers who were struggling to adapt to teaching in a pandemic.

As well, not all students have had the same access to technology with which to participate in classes remotely. Some students did not always show up for classes because there was no one home with them to keep them focused and on schedule. If they did, not all students have had the quiet space at home in which to take their classes.

These things have caused vast learning gaps for students and substantial stress, worry, and frustration for the schools and teachers supporting them.[245–248] As Ms. Ivey Welshans, a special education liaison at Middle Years Alternative School in Philadelphia, Pennsylvania, said,[249]

> *If this pandemic has done nothing else, it has glaringly shown the disparities that urban and rural districts, in particular, have been dealing with for years. The lack of technology/up-to-date technology, lack of teacher experience with technology, limited digital resources, and the lack of financial resources has hindered the ability for many school districts to quickly springboard into a digital teaching model. Many children in underserved communities have working parents who are essential workers and thus are left with little to no assistance at home. These families do not have the luxury of having parents who can afford to join forces to hire a retired teacher to run learning pods so that their parents can still work. As a result, teachers are spending their free time working with students so that they can simply access the digital class-rooms. This additional help occurs only after the teachers have spent copious amounts of time planning lessons to keep students engaged and spending boundless energy to motivate students who are highly distracted. It is the beginning of the school year, and we already feel like we would normally feel in June. We are exhausted and have serious concerns about the recoupment of skills for missed academic time and the safety of our students.*

Essential and Frontline Workers

Essential and frontline workers are those who are considered to provide essential services and, therefore, have to be present physically in-person to perform those duties.[250,251] They work in essential industries such as food service, agriculture, energy, and healthcare, and the number of these workers in the U.S. ranges somewhere between 31 and 55 million.[252,253]

Essential and frontline workers are some of the lowest paid workers in the U.S. Data from March 2020 revealed that the median hourly wage in at least half of these essential industries is less than the median hourly wage for non-essential workers. Additionally, essential workers in the food and agriculture industries specifically—at least half of whom are people of color—have the lowest median hourly wage at $13.12.[254] They also happen to be largely comprised of women, people of color, and people without a college degree.

Essential and frontline workers have been the lifeblood of this pandemic. Whether helping people with their groceries, delivering purchases from Amazon, or caring for people, they have continued to work amid the pandemic and provide people with the products and services they need to be able to live their lives and do their jobs. Remember Mr. Mande? Remember Ms. Dagrin?

It is exactly because of the essential roles they play that these workers in COVID have faced extreme challenges that many of us have not. Unlike some of us, essential and frontline workers have had to continue to go to a physical location to work instead of being able to do so remotely.

As a result, they have been more likely to be around other people and, therefore, have been at increased risk for contracting COVID.[255,256] Some studies suggest that nearly 50%—and in some cases, as many as 61%—of essential workers have been at heightened risk of severe infection.[257]

Moreover, being an essential and frontline worker does not just affect them. It also impacts their children, partners, and other family members with whom they live—and to whom they might pass the virus. One study found that dependents living with essential workers have a 17% higher risk of infection than those living with nonessential workers.[258] Because of this, these workers have had to make the hard choice between income and health—daily.

This obviously also causes great stress and worry for many of them. In fact, this group has experienced disproportionately negative mental health outcomes as a result of the pandemic, including increased substance use and elevated suicidal ideation.[259]

As we saw with Mr. Mande and Ms. Dagrin, in COVID, these workers have had to manage substantial demands, deal with interruptions to services, face challenges with financial, housing, and food security, take care of multiple people (e.g., children, parents, relatives), and face hard choices every day to balance it all.

Undocumented Immigrants

Many essential and frontline workers are undocumented immigrants and they typically work in essential sectors like agriculture, domestic work, and other service industries in the U.S. and around the globe.

These workers play an essential role in the economies of the countries and localities in which they live and work. In the U.S., there are an estimated 11 million undocumented workers, accounting for over 4% of the total workforce.[260]

Yet, despite the pivotal role they play, this is a group that is often forgotten about, and in COVID, this group has been particularly hard hit. Due to the kinds of work they typically do, they have been vulnerable to both the physical and mental health impacts of the virus as well as the economic fallout from it. For instance, an estimated four in five undocumented immigrants work essential jobs which puts them at heightened risk of contracting COVID. Additionally, they are more likely to live in dormitories or crowded apartments, which further increases their risk of exposure.

Finally, their status as "undocumented" means that they have high levels of distrust of government and institutions and are, therefore, less likely to seek help out of fear of deportation or detention. Millions of immigrant workers and families have been left largely to fend for themselves throughout the pandemic, which has led to lots of physical, mental, and economic suffering.[261]

Farm and Migrant Workers

Also falling into the essential and frontline worker category—and largely comprised of undocumented immigrants—is the farm and migrant worker community. In the U.S., there are an estimated 2.4 million farmworkers[262] and an estimated 14 million non-permanent workers.[263]

It is well established that agricultural workplaces are among some of the nation's most dangerous.[264] And in COVID, nothing has changed. While data on the risks to these workers as a result of COVID are limited due to the fact that many of them are undocumented, what evidence does exist suggests that the pandemic has exacerbated the hazardous conditions for these workers and points to high rates of infection amongst this group.[265]

Healthcare Workers

A final type of essential or frontline worker that has been substantially impacted by the pandemic is the healthcare worker (HCW)—and we have heard much about this group in terms of the negative mental and physical effects they have endured during this time. The toll that the pandemic has taken on this group has, indeed, been extensive, to put it mildly,[266,267] and they have suffered greatly.

This is a group that has seen the pandemic firsthand, up close, and from all angles. They have triaged patients. Set up field hospitals. Worn layers of PPE. Treated patients with evolving protocols as we learned how to deal with the virus better. FaceTimed with patients' families. Created whole new ICUs in unused areas of hospitals. Changed bed sheets. Fed patients. Held patients' hands. Cried with families. And, in some cases, been the only ones there to say goodbye when their patients passed away.

Additionally, they have been at high risk for COVID exposure themselves—exactly because of their roles. As of November 2020, at least 200,000 HCWs had been infected with COVID. Notably, people of color who work in healthcare settings account for the majority of these cases and subsequent deaths.[268]

They have been emotionally and physically exhausted from months of caring for others and worrying about the risks. They have put their families at-risk of infection, and this has caused additional stress and worry. Like so many others, they have struggled with parenting, caregiving, and managing everything else on their plates, and they have not necessarily been given the support they need to help them cope through this time.[269]

All of this has caused high rates of burnout, psychological stress, and suicide for this group.[270] In fact, nearly all HCWs (93%!) have reported experiencing stress over the course of this pandemic.[271,272]

Refugees and Those Seeking Asylum

As of 2020, it is estimated that there are more than 82 million people worldwide who have been forcibly displaced from their homes or home regions due to persecution, conflict, violence, human rights violations, or other events.[273] Because many of them are displaced and can be hard-to-reach, tracking the impact of COVID on this group is difficult. This also makes testing and tracing of infections and deaths hard, especially in remote areas. Therefore, data for this group are limited and the numbers that do exist are likely underreported.

Despite this, several things are known about how this group has been impacted by COVID. First, like any other group, this one has been hit hard by the virus, with infections from COVID estimated to be in the tens of thousands. As well, this group has suffered economically, as many of them rely on employment as essential or frontline workers. Finally, the data also suggest how the children in this group have suffered due to school closures and other disruptions to their education.[274–277]

People Experiencing Homelessness

On any given night in the U.S., there are an estimated 550,000 people experiencing homelessness,[278] and COVID has posed, and continues to pose, unique risks for them. The National Health Care for the Homeless Council reports that positive COVID rates can range between 9% and 12% among people experiencing homelessness.[279] Though this positivity rate is right around the average rate for the nation, people experiencing homelessness may face even more severe illnesses due to the fact that this group tends to be older and have underlying medical conditions.[280]

Additionally, as a result of COVID, support services for this community have become more limited. This is, in part, due to funding, but also, in part, due to the closures required to slow the spread of the virus.[281] These closures have made it hard for people experiencing homelessness to have access to the health and social services that they need on a consistent basis.

Finally, the pandemic has also resulted in increasing homelessness overall. Due to job and income loss, more people have experienced homelessness than ever before and many for the first time—and for those who are at-risk of homelessness, financial concerns are paramount. Often they are choosing between paying for rent, health care, food, and other basic needs.

Collectively, all of these financial burdens as well as worries about infection have been causes of increased stress and worry for this group.

Justice-involved Individuals (Formerly "Incarcerated Persons")

The pandemic has also been challenging for justice-involved individuals. In prisons, social distancing is nearly impossible, as justice-involved individuals often share cells, are crowded into communal areas for eating, and receive limited time outside.

Additionally, access to hygiene products and medical care can be unreliable. This means that such environments have been breeding grounds for the virus. Data from early in the pandemic (October 2020) revealed how nearly 140,000 justice-involved individuals had tested positive for COVID and more than 1100 had died.

While these numbers may sound low, it is highly likely that these numbers are underreported—just as with the undocumented immigrant, farm and migrant worker, and refugee communities already discussed in this chapter. This is due to the fact that testing in prison systems can be unreliable or just completely unavailable.[282–284]

Children, Youth, and Young Adults

Children, youth, and young adults have all struggled substantially amid COVID for a variety of reasons.[285–288] First, young people have been hard hit by COVID, as a disease. Whereas older adults were originally thought to be the most vulnerable to COVID, in fact, youth have been equally as susceptible to sickness and death from the virus. As of November 2021, according to CDC, there were more than 1.9 million cases of COVID infection among children 5–11 years of age, and this age group made up a greater proportion of the total number of cases.[289]

Additionally, the lingering symptoms from COVID—once thought to mostly affect middle-aged adults—have also impacted a majority of young adults.[290] As University of Dayton assistant professor of psychology Julie Walsh-Messinger, said,

> *The common belief in the U.S. is that COVID-19 is benign or short-lived in young adults. Our study, which we believe is the first to report on post-COVID syndrome in college students, almost exclusively between 18 and 21 years of age, suggests otherwise. More research needs to be done to confirm these findings, but until then, we urge the medical and scientific community to consider young adults vulnerable to post-COVID syndrome and to closely monitor those who contracted the disease for lingering viral effects.*[291]

Additionally, youth have not just been affected *physically* by COVID, they have also suffered greatly in terms of their menal health. Younger Americans have reported feeling the financial impacts of COVID acutely and have been more likely to report feeling emotional distress as the pandemic has unfolded.[292]

These experiences are even more substantial when you consider youth of color in America.[293] Food and housing insecurity have been universal experiences amongst BIPOC (Black, Indigenous, (and) People of Color) young people, with *nearly 5 million* reporting that they have had too little to eat at any given time during pandemic and *nearly 4 million* worrying about paying the next month's rent.[294]

Moreover, these experiences are not limited to youth and young adults in the U.S. We are also seeing these trends globally. In China, people under 35 have reported higher levels of anxiety and depression compared to other age groups. In Spain, 48% of 18- to 25-year-olds have reported experiencing moderate depression at the outset of the pandemic. Finally, in Slovenia, younger people have reported worse stress and mental health compared to their older counterparts. As Cécile Rousseau and Diana Miconi of McGill University write,[295]

> *[T]he COVID-19 outbreak represents an extraordinarily stressful experience for youths, including how necessary public health measures may also threaten personal and collective meaning-making, and disrupt family dynamics and youths' usual social environment.*

Finally, there have also been reports of increases in child abuse and neglect over the course of the pandemic, due to COVID-related interruptions in health care and social services. One study found that during the early days of the pandemic, especially when widespread stay-at-home orders went into effect, physical abuse of school-aged kids tripled, compared to a similar period pre-pandemic.[296] Additionally, CDC reported that the total number of emergency department visits related to child abuse and neglect that required hospitalization increased in 2020 (compared to the year prior).[297]

The LGBTQIA Community

A final group we will examine here is the LGBTQIA community, and for this group, the pandemic has also been particularly hard. This group has been especially vulnerable to COVID infection due to existing chronic conditions and risk behaviors. These existed before the pandemic too, but, as with so many other things in COVID, these have been exacerbated.[298]

This community has also been impacted severely in terms of their mental health and emotional well-being in COVID. As noted earlier in this chapter, older adults in the LGBTQIA community have struggled with loneliness and social isolation in COVID, but they are not the only ones who have experienced negative mental health challenges during this time.

Three-fourths of LGBTQIA persons (74%) say worry and stress from the pandemic have had a negative impact on their mental health.[299] As well, it has been reported how underlying mental health issues such as suicidal ideation and substance use have increased in the pandemic.[300]

Finally, like so many of the communities we have already discussed, this group has faced substantial economic impact. For LGBTQIA persons, more than half (56%) have experienced COVID-era job loss—either themselves or someone in their household.[301]

Taken together, this has meant substantial stress and hardship for members of this community in COVID.

Conclusion

At this point in the book, we have talked at length about people's experiences in COVID. I have shared some of my own and we have also explored some of the experiences of various communities of people.

Everyone has experienced COVID in some way, shape, or form, but context matters—and because of context, not everyone has experienced COVID in quite the same way.

It is important to note here that, while many of the groups that we have just discussed have struggled—I mean really struggled—these people and communities have also exhibited tremendous strength, coping, and resilience through this time. Especially, in the face of such adversity. For instance, there is documented evidence of how people of color are leveraging interpersonal connections and engagement with faith and spiritual communities to successfully cope through the pandemic,[302–304] how the Cherokee Nation has been a national leader in vaccine distribution,[305] and how the country of Uganda is engaging community organizations to share prevention and basic hygiene messages through radio, short message services (SMS), and other digital means.[306] The strengths and successes of these communities are also worth mentioning here in the context of experiences.

Moreover, there are other groups that we did not touch on here that have also struggled. Groups like arts, design, entertainment and media workers; small businesses; and transportation workers.[307] I acknowledge that the groups I have discussed here represent just some of the ones affected by the pandemic.

Finally, the struggle continues. We are not done with the pandemic yet. We are not out of the woods. And many of the experiences that people and communities have had over the last several years that we have just reviewed (namely, the metal health and eco-nomic impacts) will be the long tail of this pandemic. They will continue to linger, long after COVID becomes endemic or goes away completely (if it ever does). They will require longer-term support to address them in order for these groups to be able to successfully move forward and fully recover from the pandemic.

As we conclude this chapter, one thing is very clear—how COVID has amplified disparities between people and groups. Much of this has been felt most acutely by women and people of color, in particular, African American and Black, Hispanic/Latino, Asian American/Pacific Islander, and Tribal communities.

Moreover, such disparities are not new. They have long existed and are just now becoming a bigger part of our consciousness. As Shreya Kangovi, M.D., M.S.H.P., said,

> *COVID is a funhouse mirror that is amplifying issues that have existed forever. People are not dying of COVID. They are dying of racism, of economic inequality and it is not going to stop with COVID.*[308]

This is a big topic and therefore, is worth some more discussion. So we will turn our attention to discussing these disparities and these communities in more detail in the next chapter.

Chapter 7

Disparities Already Existed—The Pandemic Just Exacerbated Them

This pandemic has magnified every existing inequality in our society—like systemic racism, gender inequality, and poverty.

—Melinda Gates

Through my work on *How Right Now,*[309] I had the opportunity to collaborate with the Executive Director at the National Latino Behavioral Health Association, Mr. Fred Sandoval. Yes, the same Fred Sandoval who wrote the Foreword for this book.

Fred has long been an advocate for communities of color and marginalized groups. With more than 30 years of experience working in the space of health and human services, he has held numerous roles and worked with myriad communities, making him a recognized expert and trainer on culturally informed practices.

In addition to his role at the National Latino Behavioral Health Association, he has also served as a member of the SAMHSA Health Care Reform Community of Practice and on the National Council of La Raza Affiliate Council. He was formerly appointed by Governor Bill Richardson as the Deputy Secretary of Health and Income Support Division Director for the State of New Mexico and served as First Vice President of the National Alliance on Mental Illness (NAMI).

DOI: 10.4324/9781003267522-7

Fred has also worked as the Human Service Planning Supervisor for the City of Santa Fe, overseeing human services programs, and served on the National Latino Mental Health Congress during the Clinton administration.

In his work, Fred sees and interacts with people daily who struggle to make ends meet, who are having to make choices between security and safety, and who often experience disproportionately negative health outcomes. As part of our work together, he introduced me to Branda, a woman of Hispanic descent who works as a social worker in a nursing home. Branda has had a myriad of experiences in COVID and while her story is one of tremendous struggle in COVID, it is also one of hope.

It exemplifies how people have had to make hard choices in this pandemic and how COVID has not treated all of us the same. It highlights how women and people of color have been disproportionately impacted in COVID and how they have really borne the brunt of this pandemic. It also drives home the idea that context matters and that people have suffered deeply in this pandemic. It also offers glimmers of hope.

Branda's story sets us up well to have the conversation about disparities and the pandemic that we will have throughout the rest of this chapter. This is her pandemic story, and she gave me permission to share it here with you.[310]

Meet Branda

Branda is a 43-year-old woman of Hispanic descent who lives in Farmington, New Mexico. In case you are not familiar with Farmington, it is a rural city, surrounded by Navajo reservation, with a population of about 46,000 people.

Branda's homelife is full. She is married and has three children and two grandchildren. In addition to her wife, children, and grandchildren, she is close with her mother and father. They live near one another and spend a lot of time together. Her daughter stays with her parents several times a week and her mother still takes care of her grandfather, who is 90 years old. Branda's family circle comprises five generations all living together in one house or in very close proximity to one another.

Branda has been working as a social worker for 17 years, primarily with people with disabilities, and about four years ago, she started working in a nursing home.

Branda has a lot of responsibilities both in her work and home lives. At work, she cares for residents of a nursing home who go there primarily for comfort care toward the end of their lives. She works daily with people who are elderly and vulnerable, and witnessing death is a regular part of her job.

At home, Branda is a caretaker to her immediate family as well as her parents and grandfather. Her father and granddaughter are both immunocompromised, though, which means taking an extra level of precaution when caring for them. Her father has multiple sclerosis and her granddaughter was born premature with a rare lung disease called neuroendocrine cell hyperplasia of infancy (NEHI), which causes rapid and difficult breathing and low levels of oxygen in the blood in children.[311]

When COVID hit, everything changed for Branda.

People all around her in her community began to get sick. The hospitals in Farmington were overwhelmed. *Everything* at her work changed. Her nursing home immediately locked down. It stopped allowing visitors. All residents had to stay in their rooms. Everyone had to wear N95 masks. In-person dining stopped. Group activities ceased. There were no events during the holidays. And she often had to work long shifts and stay overnight at the nursing home.

Everything at home also changed. She worried about everyone in her family but especially her father and granddaughter. Everyone in the family had to be extra careful. Masks had to be worn in the house at all times. Everything had to be cleaned and sanitized (more so than they normally did). Clothes had to be changed before coming into the house. No one other than Branda went out to the stores for food and other products. Only she did that. Since she already had to go out to work, she took on that responsibility as well.

It has been *scary* for Branda. All this sickness and death. All this worry.

It also has been a really *sad* time for her.

As I mentioned, most of the residents of Branda's nursing home are there for comfort care, and, as such, arrive there either for palliative care (care during serious, complex illnesses) or for hospice care (care as people approach the end of their lives). The aim with comfort care is to provide care that is focused on symptom control, pain relief, and quality of life.[312] So the people whom Branda serves in her job often have pre-existing health conditions and are immunocompromised. They, therefore, are already vulnerable to physical and mental health stressors—like COVID.

In Branda's line of work, she deals with the realities of sickness and death all the time. In COVID, however, sickness and death have taken on new meanings for Branda. In COVID, she has been on the front lines *daily* witnessing people getting sick and dying.

Additionally, for her residents, being able to be together, do group activities, and eat meals together are things that bring them joy and happiness. When everything shut down, this was taken away, which resulted in social isolation and substantial feelings of loneliness amongst her residents.

All of this together has affected her residents and their families. They have not been able to properly say "good-bye" and mourn. And it has caused them such grief and loneliness. It has also affected Branda as she has seen all of this firsthand.

This time has also been *stressful* for Branda.

Throughout COVID, she has had to be careful about what she does in and outside of work so that she would not put her family and her residents—and herself—at any further risk. She has also had to find ways to help her family and her residents feel better and cope though this time, despite all of the challenges and limitations that they have faced.

She has also felt *frustrated*.

Namely with the panic buying: When she has not been able to find the cleaning and sanitizing products that her family required. When everyday products that she needed to keep her immunocompromised family members safe (things like water, wipes, and Lysol) quickly became unavailable. About the panic buying and shortages, she said,

> *What we needed all the time, now, everyone else needed. And there wasn't enough to go around. We couldn't get the stuff we needed. We became very angry.*

Branda has *lost a lot* in this pandemic.

She has had to make hard choices about going to work and putting herself and others at risk for infection. She has had to worry about protecting her health as well as the health and safety of both her residents AND her family.

She has had to limit her activities and her interactions with family and friends. She has taken the use of mitigation strategies such as mask-wearing, vaccination, and social distancing very seriously, but this has also meant that she has not been able to see her friends and some of her family in several years.

She has also lost people she loves during this time. One friend, in particular, had just passed away when Branda and I spoke. She had not seen him in quite a while due to the pandemic, and because of this, she missed out on telling him how much she loved him and what an amazing person he was before he died. She grieves that loss—a lot. Yes, she grieves the actual loss of her friend, but she also grieves the loss of her freedom and ability to spend time with him before he passed away. She feels robbed of that time.

She has also *seen real suffering* in her community over the course of the pandemic. Everything from people having panic attacks to seizures to car accidents. All because they were suffering and going through their own challenges as a result of the pandemic. She has tried to be there for them, when they have needed help.

Now, as we enter this latest phase of the pandemic, she is facing a new set of worries and stresses. She worries about what the relaxing of mitigation strategies and the lifting of mask mandates means for her. For her family. For her community.

Will they be ok?

Will her residents survive?

Can her granddaughter and father remain healthy as COVID continues to circulate?

All of this has taken a toll on her own physical and mental health. It has caused her a lot of headaches—and a lot of heartaches as well. She has gained weight *(haven't we all!?!)*, and she has had to go on anti-anxiety medication. And she is not sure how she will continue to manage.

It has been a hard time for her. As it has been for many people. For many of us.

Through it all, though, Branda has been a warrior.

She has made it her mission to protect her family as best as she can and tries to find humor and joy in moments with them.

She draws strength from her work and finds purpose in doing everything she can to protect her residents. She does not let anyone in her nursing home die alone and has always tried to find ways to allow families to be together and to say "goodbye," despite the mitigation measures.

Finally, she relies on her passion and compassion for others to get through this time. She has always tried to help other people with their challenges, whether physical, emotional, social, or financial—and continues to do so.

And she has not lost hope yet. She remains optimistic. For the future. For her family. For herself.

She hopes that we can learn from this experience. That we all understand how important it is to take care of one another and to do what is right to help the person next to us. She says,

If everyone takes the necessary precautions, it works.

Branda's pandemic story highlights so many of the challenges that people have experienced in this pandemic, and the choices that many people have been faced with.

Experiencing trauma, sickness, and death.

Concern about the risks of COVID.

The worry about family and infection.

The choice between work and health.

Missing hugs.

Missing being with people.

It also exemplifies the strength and sense of community that many people—facing similar situations to Branda's—have demonstrated over the course of this pandemic. That we began to discuss in the last chapter.

Most importantly, however, her story demonstrates how COVID's impact has been uneven. Depending on where you are, the kind of community you are a part of, the kind of job you do, your financial situation, and the color of your skin, COVID has affected you differently.

Context has mattered.

These inequalities are not new, though, and they did not just arrive with COVID. They have been here all along. Because of this, examining COVID's impact and these social and structural barriers a bit more is paramount. This will be the focus of the rest of the chapter.

COVID's Disproportionate Impact

The pandemic has aggravated a range of personal, social, economic, and environmental factors that contribute to individual and community health and well-being, and this has had devastating effects. As of the writing of this book,

Nearly 500 million people have contracted COVID globally.[313]

More than 6 million people have died from COVID worldwide.[314]

The median global gross domestic product (GDP) dropped by 3.9% between 2019 and 2020.[315]

More than 76 billion U.S. dollars are estimated to have been lost globally due to the pandemic.[316]

This means that the COVID pandemic has resulted in *the worst economic downturn* since the Great Depression.[317]

And we have all lived through it. But we have not all lived through it similarly.

Throughout this book, and particularly in the last chapter, we have seen exactly how different communities of people have been impacted differently—and there are data to evince this. What we have not yet covered sufficiently, however, is the impact on women and racial and ethnic communities specifically.

Here in the U.S., the pandemic has hit racial and ethnic communities much harder than white communities,[318] and this has been in terms of both their physical health[319,320] and their mental health and emotional well-being.[321–324]

According to the Mayo Clinic, American Indian or Alaska Native people are 3.1 times more likely to be hospitalized due to COVID-19 than white people, and Black/African American people and Hispanic/Latino people are both more than twice as likely to be hospitalized due to COVID-19 than white people.[325]

Additionally, as of 2021, 68% of African American/Black adults said they had experienced stress related to the pandemic and 61% reported discord in the family.[326] Mental health-related emergency room visits have also increased amongst American Indian or Alaska Native adults over the course of the pandemic.[327]

Finally, we have seen the rise of hate crimes against people of Asian and Pacific Islander descent, as they have been treated as scapegoats for COVID solely based on their race. This, of course, has caused substantial injury and death but it has also caused considerable grief, stress, and worry for this community.[328]

There have been other impacts, too. Impacts such as job, food, and housing insecurity. Hispanic/Latino adults, for example, have reported greater concern about having enough food or stable housing than any other racial or ethnic group.[329] And as we read in the last chapter, BIPOC youth have worried profoundly about food and housing insecurity in the pandemic also.[330]

Additionally, women have borne the brunt of the economic and social fallout of COVID globally, according to the United Nations. This is because women:

Tend to earn less.

Have fewer savings.

Are disproportionately active in the informal economy (economic activities not regulated or protected by nation states).

Have less access to social protections.

Are more likely to do unpaid care and domestic work, and therefore cannot participate in the labor force.

Make up the majority of single-parent households.

This relationship between physical and mental health and disruptions to basic needs is reciprocal, multidirectional, and mutually reinforcing.[331] That is, you cannot have one without the other. Like the stories of Mr. Mande and Ms. Dagrin from the prior chapter, as people struggle with access to healthy food, worry about financial security, feel forced to work in unsafe or unhealthy environments, their risk for negative health outcomes increases, and their overall health and well-being is jeopardized.

And this is exactly what has happened in COVID.

We Didn't Get Here by Accident

So *how* has this all happened? *How* have such disparities in COVID-related experiences come about? Well …

The context for how people have experienced COVID has been vastly different. Yes, here we go again: Context matters.

To better understand that context, though, we need to also understand the realities of how people have been living and working—in COVID but also before it.

The fact is that, historically, women, people of color, and other marginalized and underrepresented communities have earned less money for the jobs they do than their white male counterparts. As Pew Research Center found,

> *White men out-earn Black and Hispanic men and all groups of women.*[332]

Moreover, these groups have also historically made up the majority of the workforces in industries that have some of the lowest paid wages overall. This creates fundamental challenges for people on a number of levels. First, it makes it hard for them to be able to meet their basic needs: Things such as food, housing, and education—and that is with or without a pandemic to contend with. It also makes it hard for these communities to deal with job loss, inflation, or other similar types of challenges, as these communities do not necessarily have the requisite financial safety nets in place.

Additionally, many of the jobs that women, people of color, and other marginalized communities hold are considered essential, which requires that workers show up in-person, even in the face of a global pandemic. This puts these workers (and those with whom they live)[333] at a disadvantage when one of the best ways to protect oneself in an emergency situation like COVID is to physically distance from other people. Such realities mean that these communities face many struggles and have many worries that others do not.

Finally, in COVID, these experiences and stressors have increased and compounded. These communities have had to make the choice between health and safety and meeting basic needs. Which has caused extra pressures, anxieties, and fears.

Just like what Branda went through. Just like Mr. Mande and Ms. Dagrin.

It's Bigger Than COVID, Though

So, maybe now the *how* is clearer.

But *why* things are the way they are (and *why* things have played out the way they have in this pandemic)? Well, that is a different question. One that requires a different type of discussion.

The circumstances of COVID did not just … happen. Just as the emergence of the virus should not have surprised us, the emergence of people's particular situations in COVID should also not have come as a surprise. These are not new issues and they did not just appear overnight.

Rather, they are the direct result of the history of racism, discrimination, and marginalization that has existed and gone unaddressed for lifetimes in this country and around the world.[334–341] Further, this legacy of discrimination, racism, and exclusionary policies has left these communities without access to the necessary and appropriate resources needed to thrive.[342]

The pandemic has just brought to light the real impact of this legacy: Due to the limited social and economic resources that have been available historically to these communities, their health and well-being have been more acutely impacted by the ongoing conditions of the pandemic.[343–345] As Dr. Carolyn M. Mazure, Director of Women's Health Research at Yale University, says,

People of color are significantly less likely to have work that can be done remotely during this pandemic. The greater risk this entails is one of the many reasons why people of color are suffering greater negative outcomes of this disease, including greater health risks stemming from decades of disparity in access to equitable resources including health care. As we confront COVID-19, we must remedy the systemic inequities that continue to exist in our society.[346]

The Interplay between Social Conditions and Health—the Role of Social Determinants of Health

It is clear from our discussion thus far that social and structural conditions have contributed to people's experiences in COVID and that they have substantially impacted their health, well-being, and their ability to thrive.

The interplay between these conditions and health, though, is not specific to COVID; rather it has long existed, just setting the stage for what we have seen unfold over the course of the pandemic. Understanding the relationships between these factors and health outcomes is key to gaining a better understanding of people's lived experiences, the challenges that they face (and have faced in COVID), and *why* this is the case.

Now, I am not going to promise that this discussion will tackle all the disparities that exist in the world today or that it will even begin to answer the BIG questions about how to address the social and structural barriers that communities have faced for generations. I would never assume to think I could tackle those topics or answer those questions. I am not that expert, and this is not that book.

However, they do matter to this conversation. Therefore, I want to spend some time talking about the interplay between the conditions that can enable or inhibit positive health outcomes. In order to do this, I want to look at one major framework that has been around for more than 20 years.[347] One that many of you are likely already familiar with.

It is called Social Determinants of Health (SDOH), and it considers these social and structural conditions and applies them to health. The idea behind SDOH is that *nonclinical* factors impact a person's health—so rather than looking at just biological causes of disease, social aspects are also considered.[348–350]

Specifically, SDOH considers how both individual factors (such as race and ethnicity, gender, age, income level, education level, sexual orientation, and geographic locations) and the conditions in which people live, learn, work, play, worship, and age are linked to people's health and ability to thrive.

According to SDOH, there are five "determinants" that impact health outcomes.[351–352] See Figure 7.1:

- Economic stability (which considers issues such as employment and poverty);
- Neighborhood and built environment (which considers people's risks for things such as violence and unsafe air or water);
- Health care access and quality (which considers things such as access to recommended healthcare services and insurance coverage);
- Social and community context (which considers issues such as social connectedness and positive relationships);
- Education access and quality (which considers access to education at all levels).

Figure 7.1   The Five Social Determinants of Health.[353,354]

U.S. Department of Health and Human Services.

SDOH suggests that these social conditions—or what are called "upstream" factors—influence "downstream" factors such as health behaviors and morbidity and mortality. For example, people who do not have easy access to grocery stores with healthy foods are less likely to have good nutrition. This can result in higher risk for certain health conditions such as heart disease, diabetes, and obesity, which can lower life expectancy (compared to people who do have access to healthy foods).

Further, the body of work that supports the relationships and interactions between these conditions and health is profuse. It has explored, for example, linkages between unemployment and poor employment conditions and poor physical health and psychological distress. It also has examined relationships between discrimination (based on race/ethnicity, immigration status, and sexual orientation) and negative physical and mental health outcomes.[355–359]

This body of work signals how context really does matter. That health and well-being do not just happen in a vacuum, but that they are enabled or inhibited by the many structures and settings in which we live, work, and play. And these have been affecting people's lives—both in COVID and long before it.

SDOH and COVID—the Perfect Storm

It is important to note that while the challenges that we have been discussing—that people have been experiencing in COVID—are not new, they *have been* exacerbated in the pandemic. While disruptions to SDOH have long existed for many people, many of the particular disruptions that they have experienced in this pandemic (e.g., quarantining, shutdowns, and reduced access to services) are, in fact, unique to COVID.

The convergence of COVID, SDOH, and health outcomes has resulted in profound and noteworthy experiences for people in this pandemic. Therefore, it is worth some additional discussion to unpack this relationship a bit more. To do this, I want to take a look at the "COVID-19 SDOH Disruptions Wheel"[360] (Figure 7.2), which is a model that emerged out of research conducted in support of the *How Right Now* campaign.

The Wheel visualizes how the challenges that the pandemic has presented interact with SDOH, either supporting or disrupting them, and how these, then, lead to either positive or negative health outcomes.

At the center of the Wheel is the health outcome of interest. In this case, because the Wheel was developed out of research related to *How Right Now*, the health outcome of interest is mental and emotional health. However, any intended health outcome (whatever it may be) could be placed at the center of this Wheel.

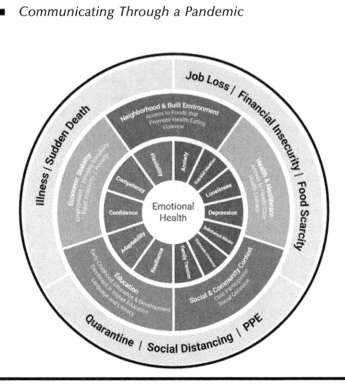

Figure 7.2   The COVID-19 SDOH Disruptions Wheel.[361]

Used with permission of Weston Medical Publishing, LLC, from How Right Now: The Role of Social Determinants of Health as They Relate to Emotional Well-Being Amidst the Covid-19 Pandemic, Burke-Garcia, Amelia, Vol 19, No 9 (2021); permission conveyed through Copyright Clearance Center, Inc.

The intended health outcome can manifest both positively and negatively (as seen in the second ring of the Wheel). In this case, there are several "positive" and "negative" dimensions of mental and emotional health that are noted in the Wheel (the positive ones are featured on the left and the negative ones on the right). For example, "Confidence" and "Flexibility" were identified as positive attributes and "Anxiety" and "Depression" were identified as negative ones. For other intended health outcomes, different positive and negative attributes would be included in this ring of the Wheel.

These dimensions of mental and emotional health are then influenced by SDOH (economic stability, neighborhood and built environment, health and health care, social and community context, and education), noted in the third ring of the Wheel. Finally, SDOH are disrupted by various aspects of the pandemic (things such as sickness, financial insecurity, and the need for social distancing), and are noted in the fourth and outer ring of the Wheel.

This Wheel exemplifies how disruptions to SDOH—brought on by COVID—can manifest positive or negative health outcomes (in this case, positive or negative impacts on people's mental and emotional health). Further, it also demonstrates how, for people who have already been experiencing disruptions to SDOH long before COVID emerged, those conditions for health and well-being (shown in the third ring) are already weakened, which makes them more vulnerable to disruptions in an emergency situation like COVID (and the resulting negative impacts on health outcomes). It clearly articulates, therefore, how the heaviest burden has been placed on those who have already been struggling.

Conclusion

The pandemic has helped shine a light on these issues, for better or for worse. It has elucidated the fact that while we have all suffered in different ways in COVID, the people who have been most affected are those who were struggling to begin with—who went into the pandemic already facing substantial challenges. They have carried the greatest burden, and they have suffered the most.

These are real people. With families. Children. Grandchildren. Parents. Communities.

Who need them. Who rely on them.

These are people who, despite such adversity, are taking steps to cope and be resilient through this time. Who are demonstrating such strength *for* their families and communities as well as *because* of them.[362]

Like Branda. And like Mr. Mande and Ms. Dagrin.

Their health and well-being affect their ability to live and thrive and provide for others. It affects other people with whom they live, work, and play. It affects their livelihoods and the economic health of their communities. And this, in turn, impacts us all. Our own health and safety. Our own economic security. And our global community and economy.

We are all intertwined. As Branda said,

If everyone takes the necessary precautions, it works.

So that everyone may thrive, we all have a role to play in helping to address these inequities and preventing disruptions to SDOH. Right now and as we look toward the future.

In March 2022, the *Journal of the American Medical Association (JAMA)* released an article on mental health-related emergency department visits in COVID, which revealed the uneven patterns in these visits amongst people of color. One of the things that the authors of that paper call for to address these disparities is the development of communication programs that are tailored to the needs and experiences of these communities.[363] This call for communication programs that can address health disparities, improve negative health outcomes, and advance a mission of health equity for all is significant.

And these are, indeed, needed. But to appreciate the context for *why* this is necessary, we need to first understand what already exists.

Remember, context matters.

Therefore, to provide this context, I now want to turn to a discussion of the communication initiatives that have rolled out over the course of the pandemic. In the next chapter, I will tell you more about the *How Right Now* campaign that I had the privilege to work on, how it was developed, and what we learned through the process of creating it. I will also review some of the other communication campaigns that have been developed during this time to try and help support people in COVID.

So, let's begin …

Chapter 8

Introducing *How Right Now* and Other Pandemic Communication Efforts

Do not let what you cannot do interfere with what you can do.

—John Wooden

As I have mentioned, the idea for this book emerged out of my experience working on the *How Right Now* campaign, as part of the U.S. response to the COVID pandemic.[364] *How Right Now* is a national communication campaign aimed at increasing coping skills and resilience for those disproportionately affected by COVID. And over the past several years, I have had the incredible honor of leading and developing this campaign—along with my team and my clients, the CDC Foundation and CDC.

The stakes were high for this project. First, we aimed to serve communities that were suffering due to the mental and emotional stressors that had been brought on by COVID. We have been exploring much of this over the course of the last couple of chapters—how people's needs have been substantial during this time and how they have only increased as the pandemic has progressed.

DOI: 10.4324/9781003267522-8

We also needed to move quickly—more quickly than I think any of us had ever moved before. The urgency of the virus meant that we did not have the luxury of time.

And we had to do this in a completely remote work environment, with a team that had never really met in-person before.

This sounds daunting. I know. It was.

But it was also *magic*. There really is no other way to describe it. There was something about this team that clicked—right from the beginning—and continued throughout the life of the project.

As I have been sharing, I have a lot of memories from these past several years in COVID, and the memories from working on this project make up a large portion of those. It was a lot of long hours. A lot of late night and early morning conversations. Lots of moments where it felt that we would never get through it all, and lots of excitement when we did.

And lots of tears. Yes, lots of them. Tears from exhaustion. Tears from stress. Tears from hearing the stories of the communities we were seeking to support. Tears of happiness as we got through different phases of the campaign. And tears for our own moments of grief, stress, fear, and worry during the pandemic. Yes, just lots of tears.

There is one memory from this time that I want to share with you that I think embodies what *How Right Now* set out to do and how impactful this campaign. This project. This moment in time has been.

For all of us who were a part of it and for all of us who have been touched by it.

But also, for me, in particular.

That memory was of the time when we were creating what would eventually become known as the *How Right Now* anthem video. An anthem video is a video that highlights a brand's or campaign's values, mission, and philosophy, and tries to convey those things by connecting with its audiences in a direct and emotional way.[365]

In creating the anthem for *How Right Now*, we wanted to achieve that emotional connection and focus on what *How Right Now* was really all about: Sharing people's experiences during the pandemic and providing support to them during this time.

To do this, we captured (remotely, of course) video testimonials of real people sharing their real stories of what they were going through in those early days of the pandemic.

These were not scripted interviews. They were not coached. They were raw. Emotional. Relevant. Heartbreaking. And they highlighted many things that all of us were universally experiencing at this time.

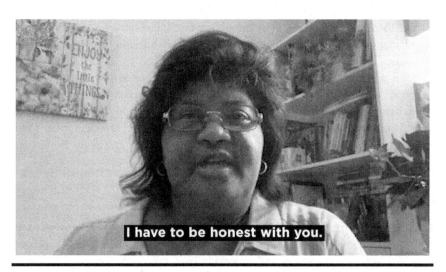

Figure 8.1   Screenshot of *How Right Now* Anthem Video.

U.S. Department of Health and Human Services/Centers for Disease Control and Prevention.

Quarantine.

Uncertainty about what was to come.

Lots of fear.

Worry for loved ones.

Anxiety about financial security.

All accompanied by the loneliness that came with everything at that time.

How Right Now was at the right place at the right time to be able to capture these experiences firsthand and share them with the world. I am so proud of this video[366] and the voices and message that it relays. See Figure 8.1.

It tells the stories of the people for whom we were building *How Right Now* in their own voices. It is authentic and honest. And as one person remarked,

It gives a voice to the voiceless.

I have already mentioned how this time was extremely challenging for me but how it simultaneously has been exceedingly gratifying. Leading the development of this campaign was a lesson in communication, in humility, in letting things go, and in leadership. I will always be grateful that I had the opportunity to be a part of this project and I am—and will always be—immensely proud of all the work that we did during this time.

Because of how special this campaign is to me and has been for me in my life, I want to share a little bit more about what it was like to work on it. So the following chapter reviews *How Right Now*, its development, what it did, and what it achieved.

But there were also many *other* campaigns that rolled out over this same time period that aimed to address urgent topics that were affecting people during the pandemic. Topics such as mask-wearing, vaccination, and social distancing.

A lot of work went into developing those other efforts as well, so I also want to spend some time looking at them. My hope in reviewing these various campaigns is that it provides a sense of all of the communication efforts that were proactively being rolled out during this time, the messages that were prominent, and how they were conducted.

Let's start with *How Right Now*.

Developing *How Right Now*

As a result of the pandemic and the associated mitigation strategies that we all have had to employ in COVID (e.g., quarantining, wearing masks), many people have had various experiences and emotions over the course of the pandemic. Some have experienced tremendous loss (e.g., loss of loved ones, freedom, jobs, and financial security). Others have experienced extreme worry and anxiety (e.g., about getting sick, about getting someone else sick, about paying bills or being evicted). Still others have experienced substantial sadness and depression (e.g., about being alone, about the state of the world, about the outlook for the future).

As a result, many people have experienced mental health challenges as they have struggled with these varying emotions since the onset of the pandemic. As early as June 2020—just a couple of months after we moved into quarantine—more than 40% of American adults were reporting negative impacts to their mental health, and the prevalence of depression was three times higher than before the pandemic.[367] Moreover, by the end of 2020, reports of anxiety and depression were *six times higher* than the previous year, with African American/Black and Hispanic/Latino communities more likely to experience such mental health challenges.[368]

People have always struggled with their mental health and their needs—in the U.S. (and around the globe)—were substantial before COVID hit. However, these challenges have only increased and gotten worse over the course of the pandemic.[369] Given such need, there was an imperative to provide resources and support in order to help address these challenges. That is where *How Right Now* came in.

Audience Research to Develop the Campaign

To inform the development of *How Right Now*, gaining an understanding of people's mental health-related thoughts, feelings, behaviors, and needs amidst COVID was critical.

To do this, we conducted rapid but robust mixed-method formative research that drew from reviews of published literature, scans of public social media conversations, needs assessment calls with partner organizations, focus group discussions, and national survey data.

And what we learned was powerful.

First and foremost, people were struggling. They were having a hard time, and they were experiencing a wide range of emotions. They wanted to know that they were not alone in their struggles. They wanted to know that it was "OK not to be OK."

Additionally, there was a deep recognition of the need to remain hopeful. They knew they were going to need to take steps to cope and find ways to be resilient through this time.

To do this, they did not want "fluffy ideas"—they wanted actionable, low-cost, low barrier-to-entry tools and resources that they could use in their everyday lives that would help them cope. Further, they wanted to receive these messages and resources through voices and channels that they trusted: Organizations that worked in their communities, celebrities whom they recognized, and social media influencers whom they followed and trusted.

It was out of this research, that the idea of *How Right Now*—or *how* do you cope *right now* in this moment—emerged. With that, a campaign was born. In both English and Spanish.

The Launch of a Campaign and How It Was Implemented

How Right Now launched on August 5, 2020, just about three months after beginning to plan for its development. Figures 8.2, 8.3, and 8.4 contain some of the campaign's creative.[370]

Figure 8.2 *How Right Now* **Campaign's "Coping" Creative.**

U.S. Department of Health and Human Services/Centers for Disease Control and Prevention.

Figure 8.3 *How Right Now* Campaign's "Listen with Compassion" Animated GIF.

U.S. Department of Health and Human Services/Centers for Disease Control and Prevention.

Figure 8.4 *How Right Now* Campaign's "Grief" Creative.

U.S. Department of Health and Human Services/Centers for Disease Control and Prevention.

One of the things that has made the campaign so special is the way in which it was rolled out. It has not used traditional mass media tactics. Rather, it has relied on those trusted sources and voices that were identified in the research to be the main channels of dissemination.

As such, the campaign has worked with organizations like Mental Health America and the National Latino Behavioral Health Association (*yes, Fred's group!*) to get the campaign's messages and resources out. It has also worked with social media influencers and celebrities like Melissa Joan Hart,[371] Omari Hardwick, Lance Bass, and Kris Jenner.[372] See Boxes 8.1 and 8.2.[373]

BOX 8.1 THE TEXT FROM MELISSA JOAN HART'S POST IN SUPPORT OF *HOW RIGHT NOW*

How are you right this very minute? Take a minute for you? With a cup of tea, good cry with a friend, 2 mile run, walk the dog, call a hotline for help, take a nap, call a family member or make sure you find someway to take a minute for you. The world can wait!! #howrightnow

View post at: https://www.facebook.com/MelissaJoanHart/posts/10157 382418471541

BOX 8.2 THE TEXT FROM KRIS JENNER'S POST IN SUPPORT OF *HOW RIGHT NOW*

It can be a challenge to cope with changing routines and anxiety during #COVID19. But we've got this. There is a way forward, and you are not alone! Visit #HowRightNow for ways that people are finding what helps: HowRightNow.org

View post at: https://www.facebook.com/KrisJenner/posts/4585575408150452

So Did the Campaign Work?

As I have said, this team and this project were just pure "*magic*." There is really no other way to put it. There are lots of reasons why this is the case (and I will get into several of them later in this book), but in part, what has made it so "magical"—and what I want to discuss here—is the fact that the campaign actually had *an impact*.

A measured positive impact. On people's ability to cope and to be resilient during this time.

Notably, data from the evaluation of the campaign revealed how it was particularly effective for those who had the greatest need, that is, those who were reporting the greatest levels of stress and discord. Further, the groups with the greatest need included people who had been suffering economically, those who had been experiencing violence, and racial and ethnic communities.

Ultimately, the campaign provided the right kind of support to the people who needed it most, exactly when they needed it.[374]

Pretty exciting, right?

I know.

I was thrilled.

And humbled.

I still cannot really believe that we did it.

That we built a beautiful campaign that has had real positive effects on people's lives. That we have done something really good in a situation that has been really bad. That people's lives were a little bit better for this campaign being in the world. Even if that impact was modest in comparison to the pandemic's toll.

It was an incredible feeling.

And it made it all worth it.

All that time spent.

All the "blood, sweat, and tears."

All those hours away from family.

All those missed dinners.

It made it all worth it.

How Right Now was not the only communication campaign that rolled out during this time, though. There have been numerous others and they have each aimed to deal with different aspects of the COVID-19 pandemic.[375] We will explore several of these next.

Other COVID-related Communication Campaigns

While *my work* over the last two years has been focused on *How Right Now*, there have been many other communication efforts that have rolled out simultaneously. Some have promoted various pandemic-related mitigation strategies (such as social distancing, mask-wearing, and vaccination). Others have addressed issues created by the pandemic (such as mental health challenges, healthcare worker burnout). Still others have addressed really difficult topics such as the rise in hate crimes against people of Asian and Pacific Islander descent that we have all been witness to in this pandemic.

These campaigns have rolled out in the U.S. as well as in other countries around the globe. We will tackle several of them throughout the remainder of this chapter but we will begin with one that rolled out at the very beginning of the pandemic. That was the *#AloneTogether* campaign.

#AloneTogether Campaign (U.S.)[376,377]

At the beginning of the pandemic—as we were all facing the newness of the virus and the pandemic along with the challenges of quarantine, shutdowns, and being socially isolated—helping people understand what to do and why to do it was paramount. Additionally, acknowledging that quarantining is hard and supporting people in their efforts to do so was also needed. It was in this context and with this understanding that *#AloneTogether* rolled out.

#AloneTogether was an initiative created through a partnership between the U.S. federal government, MTV Entertainment Group, Comedy Central, Paramount, CMT, ViacomCBS, and the AdCouncil. It was one of the first campaigns to roll out in the U.S. to support social distancing.

Launched in March 2020, *#AloneTogether* aimed to educate people on the importance of social distancing to slow the spread of the virus while simultaneously supporting people's mental health by underscoring that social distancing does not have to mean social isolation. Its core messages were focused on how:

- Social distancing helps stop the spread of COVID;
- There was no place like home to slow the spread;
- Social distancing does not mean social isolation;
- It will take every one of us to make this happen.

To promote these messages, the campaign leveraged several different types of creative assets and dissemination strategies including:

- Self-shot videos (selfie videos) created by celebrities;
- Daily engagement through celebrity posts on social media;
- A toolkit of creative assets for use by partners and the media.

Figure 8.5 contains an example of one of the campaign's creative assets.

Figure 8.5   #AloneTogether Sample Creative.[378]

Ad Council.

#BacktoSchoolTogether Campaign (U.S.)[379]

In the spring and summer of 2020, as we came out of quarantine in the U.S. and began to reopen as a nation, we looked ahead to the fall and the back-to-school time period. Unfortunately, just as we were struggling with how to safely reopen and return to some of our normal activities more generally, similar concerns were emerging as it related to students returning to university and college campuses around the country.

The *#BacktoSchoolTogether* campaign was developed in response to this. Rolled out in the U.S. in August 2020, it aimed to support students and schools as they attempted to return to normal college-life activities.

Developed through a partnership between MTV, ViacomCBS, and the Ad Council, *#BacktoSchoolTogether* aimed to promote compliance with preventative behaviors (e.g., mask-wearing, social distancing, washing hands) in school settings as well as dispel mis- and disinformation that college students were being exposed to about COVID (e.g., the effectiveness of masks, false beliefs about antibodies and immunity, the prevalence of asymptomatic spread, the significance of COVID-related symptoms). The campaign used key messages such as:

- If you have the ability, limit your contact with others;
- Wear a mask in shared spaces;
- Slow the spread of COVID.

A follow-up campaign to *#AloneTogether*, *#BacktoSchoolTogether* was similar in many ways to its predecessor. It was digital-first and featured a toolkit of creative assets that schools could easily and quickly customize for their social channels and digital platforms. Figure 8.6 shows an example of the creative from this campaign.

Stay At Home Campaign (U.K.)[380]

While all of this was going on in the U.S., across the Atlantic, the U.K. was also actively promoting a variety of mitigation strategies to its people to slow the spread of the virus.

As part of their efforts, in February 2021, the British government launched *Stay at Home*, their campaign to encourage people to stay at home, social distance, wear masks, and wash their hands. Its key messages included:

- Stay at home. Save lives;
- Stay at home. Follow the rules;
- Social distance;

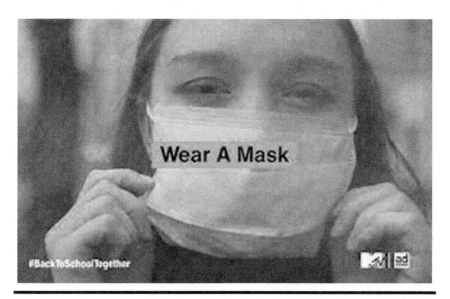

Figure 8.6   #BacktoSchoolTogether Sample Creative.
Ad Council/MTV.

▪ Continue to use other protective measures such as mask-wearing and hand washing.

This campaign was primarily disseminated via advertising spots that ran on the British television channel, ITV, as well as across radio, billboards, and social media. Figure 8.7 showcases one of the campaign's creative assets.

Figure 8.7   *Stay at Home* Sample Creative.[381]
United Kingdom National Health Service.

The #SafeHands Challenge (Global)[382]

Around the globe, similar campaigns and messages were also being seen. The *#SafeHands Challenge*, a global campaign rolled out by the WHO, is just one of them—and it is one that is still around and active today.

The campaign aims to support slowing the spread of COVID by using a number of mitigation strategies:

- Social distancing;
- Covering your cough;
- Handwashing.

Its key messages highlight how there are many practical steps everyone can take to protect ourselves and those close to us from COVID including:

- Keeping your distance;
- Sneezing into your elbow;
- Not touching your face;
- Washing your hands;
- Staying home.

It also aims to support and celebrate health care workers for their efforts during this pandemic.

Unlike the mass media campaigns that have been rolled out in the U.S., this campaign is unique in that it is primarily a user generated content (UGC) campaign. As such, it does not create a lot of its own content. Rather, it encourages people to share on social media how they are protecting themselves and their families and uses the social media hashtag, "#SafeHands," to curate people's posts.

There are also several other mini-UGC campaigns that fall under the *#Safehands Challenge* umbrella campaign:

- A Handwashing Challenge, which asks people to record a video following the WHO guidance about handwashing and share it on social media;
- The #HealthyAtHome Challenge, which asks people to share the healthy habits they are doing at home;
- The #ThanksHealthHeros campaign, which asks people to share short messages of support to nurses, midwives, and other health care workers around the world on social media.

The WHO's campaign has been supported by people from all around the world, including WHO Goodwill ambassador and soccer player, Alisson Becker, the current

Figure 8.8 Sample Creative from the *#SafeHands Challenge* Campaign.[383]
World Health Organization.

President of Rwanda, Paul Kagame, and actor, Selena Gomez. Figure 8.8 features an example of one of the few pieces of creative that the campaign developed itself.

"It's Up to You" Campaign (U.S.)[384]

While messages of social distancing, hand washing, and mask-wearing were being widely disseminated—in the U.S. and around the globe—vaccines started to become available. During this time however, it was becoming clear that a massive effort was needed in the U.S. to raise awareness of the vaccine, answer people's questions, quell fears, and encourage as many people as possible to make the choice to get vaccinated.

This has been the aim of the *"It's Up to You"* campaign, which has been one of the largest public education efforts in U.S. history. Created by the COVID

Collaborative[385] in partnership with CDC, *"It's Up to You"* launched in February 2021 with the aim of helping people—particularly people of color—feel confident about getting vaccinated by listening to their questions, hearing their concerns, and working to educate and empower people to make informed choices about vaccination for themselves and their families.

The campaign's key messages are:

- Make an informed decision about COVID vaccination for yourself and your family;
- Have questions about COVID vaccines? Here's where to start;
- Get the latest information about COVID vaccines;
- Be confident in the COVID vaccine;
- Get vaccinated once a vaccine is available;
- Get boosted.

The campaign includes a variety of creative assets both in English and Spanish *(as well as in seven other languages!)* and has been rolled out using a mix of organizational partners, media, and other trusted voices (faith leaders, medical experts). Figure 8.9 shows an example of the creative from this campaign.

Figure 8.9 "It's Up to You" Sample Creative.[386]

Ad Council.

#YoMeVacuno Campaign (Chile) [387–389]

Just as the U.S. was trying to figure out how best to promote the COVID vaccine to its people, the country of Chile was also tackling this critical issue. In response to this, the Chilean Ministry of Health developed its COVID vaccination campaign, *#YoMeVacuno*, and it had one primary aim: To vaccinate as many people as possible.

It has, in fact, been one of the standout campaigns for getting people vaccinated—worldwide.

Chile's campaign has not been like any of the other campaigns we have explored thus far, though, as it did not develop creative assets or use the media or celebrities to disseminate messages. Rather, this campaign was focused on the operational aspects of getting people vaccinated and bringing the vaccines to where people naturally congregate in order to make it as easy as possible for them to do so.

As part of this campaign, the Chilean Ministry of Health took several key steps:

1. It set up vaccination sites at universities and stadiums;
2. It published a calendar that clearly stated who is eligible for a vaccine and on what day;
3. It did not require appointments;
4. It maintained a robust national immunization registry to track when people got their shots and when they would be due for another dose, no matter where they were located in the country.

The Ministry also gave out #YoMeVacuno ("I got vaccinated") cards to people after vaccination, and many people started posting pictures of themselves with these cards on social media using the hashtag #YoMeVacuno. Figure 8.10 shows an example of #YoMeVacuno creative.

Figure 8.10   Sample Creative from Chile's #YoMeVacuno Campaign. [390]

Ministry of Health of Chile.

"Mask Up America" Campaign (U.S.)[391]

As the vaccine rollout in the U.S. ramped up around the summer of 2021, the mask debate also started to intensify again around that same time. *(Remember our discussion from Chapter 5 about the reversal on mask-wearing guidance when it became clear that vaccinated people could still spread the virus?)*

Thus, it became clear that something needed to be done to highlight the importance of mask-wearing—regardless of whether or not someone was vaccinated. This was the context in which the *"Mask Up America"* campaign was developed.

Created through a partnership between CDC and the Rockefeller Foundation, the campaign launched in July 2021 and aimed to promote the wearing of masks and other face coverings to slow the spread of COVID.

The campaign offered numerous creative assets for partners and the media to use, including public service announcements (PSAs) in English and Spanish. These featured celebrities such as WNBA star, Elena Delle Donne, and Isabella Gomez (from One Day at a Time), and aired in completely donated broadcast, digital, and audio media time and space across the country.

The campaign also leveraged milestone events, such as the Olympic Games and live concerts, to highlight how wearing masks can help us safely return to doing some of the things we love (but that we had been unable to do in COVID). Figure 8.11 features an example of the creative from this campaign.

Figure 8.11 "Mask Up America" Sample Creative.

Ad Council/ISDA.

#StopAsianHate Movement (U.S.)[392,393]

Finally, while these other campaigns were rolling out and addressing direct effects of the virus by promoting social distancing, mask-wearing, and vaccination; by dispelling myths and misinformation about the virus and related preventive behaviors; and by addressing the mental health challenges that had arisen over the course of the pandemic, other consequences of COVID were emerging that needed to be addressed.

Darker and more reprehensible ones. Arguably, some of the worst we have seen in this pandemic.

I am talking about the rise in hate crimes across the U.S.

The FBI defines a hate crime as a,

> *Criminal offense against a person or property motivated in whole or in part by an offender's bias against a race, religion, disability, sexual orientation, ethnicity, gender, or gender identity.*[394]

And in COVID—since the first reports of a new virus in China emerged in 2019—we have seen increases in these types of crimes, in particular, against people of Asian and Pacific Islander descent. As people across the U.S. sought to blame someone for COVID, they have lashed out at groups that they have mistakenly held culpable—and people of Asian and Pacific Islander descent have been a main target for this kind of hatred and violence. In fact, reports of hate crimes against people of Asian and Pacific Islander descent jumped 124% between 2019 and 2020 and further increased (*by 342%!*) between 2020 and 2021.[395]

As a result of this, numerous campaigns and grassroots efforts have emerged to try and address this reality and stop such hate crimes from happening. A notable one I want to mention here is called *#StopAsianHate*, which began after the killing of Vicha Ratanapakdee in January 2021[396] and intensified in the wake of the mass shooting at three Atlanta spas just two months later.[397]

#StopAsianHate refers to several anti-Asian-violence rallies that have been held across the U.S. in response to the hatred, racism, and violence against Asian Americans and Pacific Islanders related to the pandemic. The movement's main messages are:

- Read about the current crisis of anti-Asian hate and violence;
- Raise awareness by sharing information with the media and your social networks;
- Commit to anti-racist action by volunteering, donating, and advocating for all marginalized people.

The movement houses numerous resources and information on its website: www.stopasianhate.info and uses social media to curate information, data, and visual content using the hashtag, "#StopAsianHate."

Many social media users use this hashtag to share their own experiences with racism and call on their followers to speak up and stand up for those who are affected by and vulnerable to such racist violence.

In addition, many celebrities and artists have spoken out to raise awareness about the increase in hate crimes targeting Asian and Pacific Islander communities over the course of the pandemic.

Conclusion

Throughout this chapter, we have talked a lot about my campaign (if I can call it that), *How Right Now*, and we have also spent some time looking at some other campaigns that have rolled out around the same time. Collectively, these campaigns have sought to address some of the biggest issues that we have faced as a global society over the past several years.

Social distancing.

Mask-wearing.

Hand washing.

Loneliness and mental health.

Vaccination.

Mis- and disinformation.

Return to school.

Return to regular activities.

Violence.

Racism.

Hate crimes.

Each of them has had a big job to do and a tough environment in which to do it. Further, each of them was created in environments in which we were mostly, or entirely, remote. With teams and collaborators who likely did not know each other that well—if at all.

While I can tell you about some of the key elements of those other campaigns, what I cannot tell you about is what happened behind the scenes with each. The inner workings of them. How the teams put them together. How they worked together as a team. How they managed to build these initiatives in remote environments. What motivated them. Whether they thought that they were successful. Whether their campaigns have had a measured impact. Whether it was satisfying for those involved—maybe even enjoyable in some cases.

For those other campaigns, I cannot answer those questions for you, but I can tell you about these things as they relate to *How Right Now*. I did see the inner workings of the *How Right Now* team firsthand, and I can tell you, it was not easy.

Building and leading a team … in a completely remote environment. Where many team members had never met in-person. With such a large goal and huge stakes. And on such a fast timeline was …

Difficult.

Overwhelming.

Maybe a little insane?

But it worked. Like magic.

I can speak to how it all came together. And what I learned through it all. I can give you that "peek-behind-the-curtain." So that is what I want to explore with you next.

Chapter 9

Building a Team and a Communication Campaign in the Middle of a Global Pandemic

To successfully work with other people, you have to trust each other. A big part of this is trusting people to get their work done wherever they are, without supervision.

—*Sir Richard Branson*

While *How Right Now*[398] is one of my more recent experiences working on and leading a national communication campaign, it is not my first. My experience working on these kinds of communication-related projects spans 20 years and one of my first experiences—ever—doing this kind of work happened early in my career. It was about 14 years ago and I was part of a team that was tasked with planning, organizing, implementing, and evaluating CDC's National Influenza Vaccination Campaign.[399]

This campaign is an annual effort to help raise awareness about the flu and the importance of getting vaccinated against it.[400] To support this campaign, various communication strategies and tactics have been used over the years including:

DOI: 10.4324/9781003267522-9

- Media buys;
- Media round tables;
- Television and radio PSA creation and pitching;
- Print and advertorial placements;
- Partner engagement;
- Social media content development and dissemination;
- And more recently, newer tactics such as using celebrity and social media influencers.

Figures 9.1[401] and 9.2[402] highlight examples of campaign creative that have been developed over the years. Figure 9.1 is from 2011 (when I actually ran the campaign) and Figure 9.2 is from the most recent iteration of the campaign in 2021 *(nearly 10 years apart!)*.

One of the cornerstone moments for this campaign is National Influenza Vaccination Week (NIVW),[403] which takes place annually, usually during the first full week of December. When I worked on the campaign, it was during this week that the majority of the campaign's promotional activities would happen. Plans for NIVW typically included a myriad of activities such as:

Figure 9.1   CDC's National Influenza Vaccination Campaign Creative (2011).

U.S. Department of Health and Human Services/Centers for Disease Control and Prevention.

Figure 9.2 CDC's National Influenza Vaccination Campaign Creative (2021).
U.S. Department of Health and Human Services/Centers for Disease Control and Prevention.

- Paid media placements across digital, print, and radio (depending on the year and the budget, sometimes there were also Out-of-home (e.g., billboards) and television placements);
- PSAs on radio and television;
- Numerous partner engagements and activations;
- A number of media briefings and roundtable interviews with CDC spokespeople;
- Virtual events and social media activations such as TwitterChats and webinars;
- And finally, a large press conference hosted by The National Foundation for Infectious Diseases (NFID), which usually included someone of prominence (in most cases, it was the President of the United States) getting their flu vaccine.

NIVW was all consuming—it was kind of like the campaign's Superbowl.

Given the intensity of NIVW, you can imagine how much planning went into getting ready for it every year. We developed an NIVW plan. We held regular team status meetings and check-ins with our CDC clients. We developed new messaging, creative, products, and resources. We drafted and confirmed media buy plans. We outreached to and engaged partners. We planned events and lined up celebrities and other trusted voices to help with promotion.

Then, as NIVW kicked off, the "real work" started. We had to stay on top of and coordinate all of the various time-oriented and fast-paced tactics that we had been planning. We were in touch with partners and vendors daily, confirming plans, activities, and creative. We were ensuring that paid media placements went live on time. We were verifying that our planned activities were happening on schedule and that the right people were in attendance. And we were identifying issues as they arose and addressing them swiftly.

There were a lot of moving pieces to NIVW and we had to be sure that everything went off without a hitch. So to keep us on track, the team got into the habit of holding daily stand-up meetings during NIVW. These were daily meetings we had at the outset of each day for 15-30 minutes. We would meet first thing in the morning and review the plans for the day. Each team member would quickly report out on the status of their tasks, noting any challenges or issues that needed to be addressed. Finally, key action items that needed to be tackled were identified. These meetings served to help the team review deliverables, stay on task, and address problems quickly.

And they paid huge dividends. These daily stand-ups brought us together. Regularly and often. They kept us on task. They ensured that everyone felt included. They helped cement roles and responsibilities for the day and for the week overall. They helped alleviate tensions and prevented issues from becoming bigger.

Ultimately, they helped make us a team.

Fast forward almost 20 years later and I have been tasked with leading the development of the *How Right Now* campaign. We reviewed in Chapter 8 how this was an incredibly fast-paced, intense, high-stakes project with an insane timeline for launch. Given this, as we set out to build what would eventually become *How Right Now*, one of the first things I implemented was daily stand-up meetings.

Because we were moving so quickly and this project was so big with so many pieces, meeting daily to review the status of items and deliverables, address issues, approve things, raise questions, and make plans for what we needed to accomplish that day was the only way I could see us accomplishing everything we needed to. Particularly in the time frame in which we needed to do it.

And just as these meetings were incredibly valuable for the team working on NIVW all those years ago, so were they for the *How Right Now* team twenty years later. They helped us stay focused, keep to our timelines, and address issues swiftly. Because these meetings included CDC and the CDC Foundation, they also allowed for close coordination with our clients on a daily basis. This, ultimately, helped ensure alignment on project tasks and deliverables and avoid unnecessary conflict and tension.

They helped us form a strong team very quickly—and I truly believe they contributed substantially to the success of the project.

I have already mentioned how *How Right Now* was developed in a completely remote work environment where most of the team members had never met in-person before. Therefore, the unique challenge for this particular project was to build a cohesive team—rapidly. This was the only way we were going to be able to successfully bring this campaign to life on the timeline that was required.

But how do you do that when you do not know one another and you cannot get together in person?

It is hard. Or I should say, it is harder. But it can be done.

And this team did it. Despite the remote work environment and not being able to get together in-person, we came together and formed a cohesive team that accomplished its goals—and the daily stand-ups helped with this. They brought us together first thing every morning, provided a mechanism through which to address issues quickly, enabled communication when we were exhausted and at the ends of our ropes, and helped us stay focused on our common goal.

What is so interesting to me about this, though—and why I wanted to share this story with you—is that I do not think that I was really cognizant at the time about exactly where the idea for those daily stand-ups came from … I just proposed we have them.

It was really only upon reflection when I realized where I got the idea—from an experience I had had 20 years ago. That same strategy that proved invaluable almost two decades ago did the same thing for this team years later.

It is important to note, though, that the successful functioning of this team was not just due to the daily stand-ups. It was not just these meetings that made this team come together. Yes, they were a part of it but there was something else. Despite the fact that most of us had never worked together and had never met in-person, this team was magical. It just worked. It worked *so well*.

Now, I am not a management expert or an expert in team building or coaching. There are people who have spent their whole lives refining the knowledge and approaches in that space—and I am not one of them. Nor is this book meant to be a book on team management. There are already many, many good ones out there on that topic. This book is about communicating through a pandemic.

Still, team management and communication have been pieces of my experience over these last few years. They are part of my pandemic story. So I do want to talk about what it was like to lead and manage a team in this environment; through a pandemic; with a tough job to do; and completely remotely. Thus, it is worth unpacking our process and our team a little bit more for you. This will be the focus of the remainder of this chapter.

Principles of Team Development and Management

Before I jump into my experiences and learnings from working on *How Right Now* over the course of the pandemic, I want to share some fundamentals and best practices from the world of team development and management with you to help contextualize my own story.

The literature is rich with this kind of information. There are many principles, fundamentals, and best practices from which to draw, but one primary principle that resounds across numerous articles and studies is that having a successful team does not just mean that you have talented people.

Yes, of course, you need to start with this. Sure. You need talented and capable people to do the work well. But almost every leader will tell you that staffing is not the way to build a good team.[404,405] Rather—and I am summarizing from multiple sources here—strong teams generally have the same five qualities:

- A common purpose;
- Clear goals;
- Often and regular communication;
- Respect;
- They say, "thank you".

I discuss each of these in more detail below.

Having a Common Purpose[406,407]

Having a common purpose has to do with the commitment of the people on your team to the thing you are striving to do—what motivates them and what drives them to see the project through to its completion. Helping others. Enacting social change. Making life a little better in some way for people.

Having a common purpose is distinct from goal setting (which really has more to do with identifying the things that need to be completed, e.g., develop a policy, build an app, work a phone bank).

Yes, they might be linked, but purpose goes deeper. You need the "purpose" before you can "set the goals."

Establishing a team's common purpose is a matter of asking yourself,

What are you trying to change?

What are you trying to improve?

Whatever it is, it is the vision for the team. It is the "heartbeat" of the team, and I think every well-functioning team has to have their "heartbeat" first. No matter what the goal.

Setting Clear Goals[408,409]

Once the "heartbeat" for the team has been identified, then that goal setting can begin. Setting appropriate and clear goals includes things such as:

- Clarifying deliverables;
- Assigning responsibilities;
- Confirming deadlines and milestones;
- Allocating resources, e.g., time, materials, space, and money.

Goal setting is very important to the functioning of the team because it helps ensure that all team members know what they are responsible for and how they are going to complete their tasks. As such, goal setting adds value at multiple levels of team functioning—the team as a whole, its managers, and individual team members.

At the *team* level, goal setting helps clarify what the team is there to do and how they will do it: Develop a product, launch a website, raise a certain amount of money, pass new legislation. Whatever it is, the team has to know what it is there to accomplish. They also need to agree upon the path the team will take to accomplish the goals. This means setting a timeline within which to do the work and meet deadlines.

At the *manager* lever, goal setting helps carve out clear roles and "swim lanes" for individuals on the team. Managers need to understand the strengths of their team members and find roles that accentuate those. Setting goals for team members helps to articulate what their roles are and helps managers ensure that the division of labor makes sense and is understood. It can also help managers obtain input and buy-in from their team members on timelines, deliverables, and deadlines.

Finally, at the *individual* level, it is critically important that we, as members of a team, understand our unique roles and responsibilities both *as part of* that team as well as *to* other members on that team. Setting clear goals at the *individual* level certainly requires work to be done at the *manager* level, but it also requires that individuals, themselves, be active participants in this process. They need to think about their role on the team and on the project and take time to self-reflect on what they bring (their strengths) to the team and what they need to improve (their weaknesses) to help make the team better. Goal setting can help ensure that we, as individuals, understand where we fit in and how we are meant to contribute to the team in order to ensure its success.

Communicating Often and Regularly[410,411]

Communication is critical to a team's success; but team communication is not just about meetings or emails. Yes, those are, of course, important, but team communication is so much more than that.

Team communication helps with *building* the team. It helps establish the team vision and establish its goals. It is a means by which a team can monitor and review its progress, identify successes and challenges, and discuss how to address issues. Communicating often and regularly will help ensure that expectations are being set and reinforced within the team and managed and adjusted as the project moves along.

Each team has its own way of communicating, so the methods and modes that work for one team will differ from what works for another. What is universal across teams that communicate successfully, though, is that they have figured out the *style of communication* that works best for their team.

To figure out the *style of communication* that works best for your team, you want to consider several things. First, you want to consider how *homogeneous* your team is. Do you all come from similar backgrounds, cultural orientations, and speak the same language? Do you all work for the same organization or are you from different organizations with different company cultures? Is the team comprised of individuals who see and express things similarly or differently?

You also want to consider the physical *proximity* of your team. Is your team located all together in one place or are they dispersed? Are they all in one time zone or are they spread out across multiple? Do they meet in-person (or would they, were we not still in COVID?) or is your team's main way of connecting via technology?

Finally, you want to consider the *communication preferences* of your team members. Do your team members all prefer to communicate in the same way, using the same modes, and with the same styles? Or is communicating with some people better face-to-face while others on the team prefer text-based written communication?

It is highly likely that, in this day and age, any team you lead or are a part of will be comprised of people: Who are from different backgrounds, who express things differently, who are both in-person and remote, who may work for different organizations, and who prefer different types and modes of communication. Therefore, leading and being a part of such diverse teams will require nimble and adaptive ways of communicating, as you learn what works best—both for the team as a whole and for the individual members of that team.

Regardless of the *style of communication* you choose for your team, what is important to remember is that communication should be open, frequent, and regular. At the end of the day, team building is all about relationship building, so while meetings, calls, emails, texts, and in-person visits offer great opportunities for the team to come together on logistical and operational tasks, they also are ways to help build bonds within the team. To aid you in your journey to communicate more effectively with your teams, several principles of effective team communication can be found in Box 9.1.

BOX 9.1 PRINCIPLES FOR EFFECTIVE TEAM COMMUNICATION

Meet regularly. Unless you are working on a project with a tight timeline, daily meetings are likely not necessary, but regular meetings still are. Think about the cadence with which you will meet and discuss things with your team.

Encourage the use of video for teams that are dispersed. This will help make people feel like everyone is together even if they are not in the same room.

Allow people NOT to use video when they need a break from it. "Zoom fatigue" is real. We have all been there in this pandemic. So give people a break sometimes. Let them know that being on camera, while encouraged, is not required.

Be present and listen to your team members. When your days are filled with endless Zoom and Teams meetings, it can be enticing to quickly check email or respond to a text while on a call. And multitasking has become a way of life for us in the pandemic—I know I am completely guilty of this, and likely you are too. But it is incredibly important to team communication and development to tune in, be present, and participate in the conversations that are happening.

Keep an open mind and make space for discussion and debate about ideas. Allow team members space for ideation and sharing. Even if an idea will not work well because of timing, budget, or context, be appreciative of your team members for sharing their ideas. You do not want to squash creativity because you never know where the next great idea will come from.

Find other ways to touch base and stay in contact with your team. Communication does not just happen in meetings—it can also happen in a variety of other ways. A quick call to someone or stopping by someone's work space for a quick visit (if you can be there in-person) can be a nice way of saying "hello" and checking in. A quick text message or email that expresses appreciation for something someone has done well is a nice way to reinforce roles and let your team members know that you see them and the effort they are putting in.

Respecting Each Other[412,413]

We just mentioned how, in today's world, each team will likely be comprised of many different types of people—with differing lived experiences and viewpoints and unique perspectives. While this can create challenges, it is actually the best way to design a team. You want members with complementary skills and abilities and who can bring a diverse range of viewpoints and ideas to the table. This can allow for harmonious work, as well as the freedom to challenge each other when necessary (if supported correctly).

Of course, diverse teams can also have their challenges—because people do not always see eye-to-eye or fully understand each other. But this is where the principle of "respecting each other" comes in. This principle does not just have to do with "showing respect" to someone; rather, it involves supporting and trusting one another.

"Respecting each other" means acknowledging when there is a challenge and supporting your team members when someone is struggling or something is not working well or as it was intended. The deftness to acknowledge these issues, make swift changes to address them, not get sidetracked with emotion when something does not work out, and course-correct to get the project back on track help show respect for the team. It helps ensure that the team is functioning at its best so that it can be successful. So that it can move forward and achieve its goals.

Saying "Thank You"[414,415]

Finally, showing gratitude to your team members is key to building a strong team culture. It helps build morale and motivates team members to push forward and continue to do their jobs well—especially if working under intense circumstances.

Saying "thank you" can happen at the *team* level or the *individual* level and can take the form of a verbal shoutout in a meeting, an email to a staff person with a cc to their manager, or some kind of team celebration like a lunch or dinner out (again, if and when people are gathering in-person). These signs of appreciation should happen consistently and regularly enough so that your team members feel rejuvenated and motivated in the work they are doing. Regardless of *how* you say, "thank you," taking the time to recognize, reward, and celebrate your team and your team members is vital to building a strong team.

A Few Final Notes on the Principles of Team Building

The tenets that we have just reviewed are applicable to any team and in any work environment. While some of them may be more oriented toward being a leader or manager of a team, they can apply to being a team member as well.

Believing in the work you do and feeling that you are a part of a team's common purpose help *all* team members feel like they matter and that their contributions make a difference. Asking for, clarifying, and sticking to the goals set out early on can help you feel like you know what you should be doing and that you are playing your part in the team's success. Communicating openly and honestly can help you address issues early and more easily achieve your goals. And, showing respect for and acknowledging your team members' efforts will help you build stronger relationships with your colleagues and can contribute to the team successfully achieving its goals.

Finally, it is worth noting that these are not easy things to do. They take patience and discipline. They require thought and effort. But they are vital to building a strong and successful team. They contribute to the "heartbeat" and they help a team achieve its goals. And they help ensure that the team's vision is achieved and that team members feel as if they have been part of something greater.

So that is Team Building and Management 101. *Amelia-style.*

Pandemic or no pandemic.

And yes, while these principles do apply whether or not you are working as part of a team in a pandemic, this is a book about communicating through a pandemic. And COVID has certainly changed our world. All of our worlds (personal and professional). Quite. A. Bit.

Which has impacted how we work.

The quarantining and social distancing that the pandemic has required of us have forced many of us to do things differently than we did them before COVID. This has meant that we have had to learn to build teams, create unified visions, and solidify bonds remotely. In some cases, we have had to do these things with team members we have never met in-person before.

Even with the pandemic easing a bit at different points and some people returning to their offices, this trend of remote work seems likely to continue, in some way, shape, or form into the future. Given this, some of the tenets we have just discussed may need to be adapted for full-time remote team members—some may become more difficult in this new environment while others may become easier.

To the former—*team building principles that have become harder in remote work environments*—consider, for a moment, how the casual act of swinging by someone's office to say "hi" and check-in has been virtually eliminated because of COVID. Many of us have not gone into an office space in more than two years, and even for those of us who have, we do not gather together like we once did. Those office visits and acts of collegiately that we once did so casually, are now done more often over Zoom or phone (or not done at all).

The ability to run into someone in a break room or large staff meeting and chat about an idea, unplanned and unscheduled. Well, that just does not happen when staff are working remotely. Those "watercooler" conversations have become quite rare since COVID.

As well, getting together for a lunch to say "thank you" has, in COVID, most often turned into a scheduled Zoom meeting. Even if people do try and get together in-person, comfort levels with being in-person and going out to restaurants must now be taken into consideration.

However, it is not *all* bad. To the latter category—*team building principles that have become easier in remote work environments*—consider the growth in the number of technologies that enable faster, more regular, and more frequent connections and collaboration opportunities and spaces. There are now more ways than ever before to communicate, connect, and see each other's faces—and this does help teams with remote members connect and build bonds despite the barriers of time and space.

Knowing that this trend of remote work is likely to continue, finding virtual ways to establish collective visions, set and manage expectations, build and deepen relationships, ensure that team members are on the same page, and do these things over time, will be crucial to the success of teams and projects into the future.

Ultimately, we must get creative about how we do "team building" in this new world. We need to continue to invest in building these kinds of relationships—for the success of our projects and our people. And we need to be open to using a variety of approaches—virtual and non—to do so if we want to be successful.

Building and Leading a Team in a Pandemic

With these tenets of successful team building, and the context of how team building has shifted substantially as a result of COVID, clear in our minds, we can now turn back to a deeper discussion of team building as it relates to the *How Right Now* campaign.

To start, let me share a little bit about who comprised the team. First and foremost, the *How Right Now* team was big. It was comprised of more than eighty staff from across three different organizations (NORC at the University of Chicago and its partners, Burness Communications, and TMN Corp) and two clients: CDC and the CDC Foundation (both of whom were actively involved in the development of this campaign). We also worked with several different partners and vendors over the course of the campaign.

The team was also diverse. We had people from all racial and ethnic backgrounds on the team. We had team members who lived all over the country. We also had several team members for whom English was not their first language. Finally, we had people with decades of experience (20 years+) on the team as well as people who had just entered the workforce.

Finally, the team was interdisciplinary. As such, it included people with expertise in various disciplines including qualitative and quantitative research, statistics, data visualization, health communication, evaluation, translation and transcreation, mental health and clinical psychology, cultural communication, writing and design, digital and social media, partner outreach and engagement, and project management.

So what exactly was it about this team—and how we functioned—that worked so well? How could a team that had mostly never met in-person work so seamlessly together?

If we think back to what is in the literature on best practices for team development and management, I think there are a number of attributes of the *How Right Now* team that align with those principles and which helped contribute to its success.

To start, of course, everyone on the team was *capable and qualified*. There were never many issues pertaining to work quality or inexperience. We know, though, that having qualified people on your team—while a necessity for success—is not enough to create a well-functioning and successful team. So this was just our foundation.

Adding to this was the fact that everyone on the team really liked each other as people and as colleagues. There was, from the beginning, a *mutual respect* for each other—for our individual skills and accomplishments, as well as for what each of us brought to the team and the project.

There also was a *common purpose*. Everyone on the team was driven to help people. It was what motivated us and what got us up in the morning. We all had chosen to work for organizations—including our clients, CDC and the CDC Foundation—that were committed to doing this kind of work. Work that aimed to serve others. And we all cared about public health and improving people's lives.

It was just part of our DNA.

You could feel this sense of commitment throughout the team—at all levels and from every single team member, no matter what role they were playing. Including our clients. No matter what time of day or night it was, they were willing to talk something through, discuss an idea, make something happen. Everyone—and I mean everyone—really cared about the project and the success of it. We all felt that we were striving to achieve something really important and meaningful.

We also were all in "it." We were all experiencing COVID firsthand, and this strengthened our "common purpose." Some of us knew people who got COVID. Some of us got COVID ourselves. Some of us knew people who died from COVID. Some of us were challenged mentally and emotionally—not just because of the work, but because of the whole pandemic situation. Some of us had children at home, popping into meetings, needing something, or wanting attention. Some of us had dogs who needed to go out at the most inconvenient times or cats who walked across computer screens.

We all had full plates. Overflowing plates. And we were all trying to manage all of it.

It was exactly in this context that we were brought together to work on a project that was focused on some of those same issues caused by that same pandemic. We were all living "it" as we worked on "it."

As a result, we all connected to the aims and vision for this project easily and quickly. We knew we had a job to do, and we were aligned in terms of what that job was: Designing a campaign that would help people who were struggling at this critical moment in our world's history.

In some ways, we were building this for ourselves.

And *that* was our singular "heartbeat."

Because of this "common purpose," we were able to *identify and set goals* quickly and easily. Team members had clear roles and responsibilities. Some people were responsible for research. Others for messaging and creative. Some were part of data analysis. While others were in charge of working with partners. Whatever their role was, everyone knew what they had to do and on what timeline they had to do it.

And those daily stand-ups? Yes, they helped us stay on track and achieve those goals, but they also enabled *frequent and regular communication* across the team on a daily basis. They often resulted in subsequent meetings to discuss things that came up in the stand-ups. They led to email or phone call follow-ups on items that specifically needed to be addressed. They generated quick questions over text message and Teams or Skype pings to clarify things. They were the foundation from which all other communication within the team flowed.

Finally, we tried to *celebrate our successes* and say "thank you" as much as we could. As you can imagine, this was perhaps one of the harder things to do in a pandemic where we could not get together in-person. But we tried. We acknowledged small successes like the development of our anthem video (that we discussed in Chapter 8), and we celebrated virtually as a team when the campaign officially launched. I sent flowers to key members of my team who pulled all-nighters and maintained intense schedules in the early days of the project. We submitted for external industry awards for the campaign *(of which the campaign won many!)*.

And finally, one day, after so many months of hard work and long days, and after everyone was vaccinated, we did get together for a dinner (outside at a restaurant) to celebrate and to meet for the very first time. We finally had the chance to meet some of our colleagues in-person. It was amazing and so, so gratifying.

The literature says that in order to build a successful team, we should have a "common vision," set "clear goals," have "regular and frequent communication," have "respect for one another," and say "thank you." I think this team did that, not because that is what the literature says we should do, but because it is what felt right and made sense to this group of people working on this project at this moment in time.

It was magic. And it was incredible.

And we honestly had a great time—in a time that was really quite terrible. We learned lots of things from one another, which was refreshing and interesting, and people had great attitudes despite being in a really rough situation.

I have said it before, and I will say it again, leading this team and this campaign has been the honor of my career. If I never do another thing in my career, I will always hold this time and this body of work in a special place in my heart.

Conclusion

So here we are, almost at the end of the book. We have covered a lot thus far but we have one more stop to make before we wrap up. As we close out this book, I think it is worth taking a step back and examining everything we have already discussed and what it all means. So in the next—and last—chapter, I want to summarize what we have covered, talk a little bit about what we have learned, and think a little bit about where we go from here.

With this in mind, the final chapter of this book will begin with a brief review of the topics we have discussed in this book and highlight some key takeaways. Then, based on these learnings, I propose a vision for the future of pandemic communication.

Now, I am not going to pretend to know what it is like to be on a national or global pandemic response team full-time. Day-in, day-out. For more than two years. The intense timeline. The struggles. The communication challenges. The backlash and anger. The pressure to address major health issues impacting people in the U.S. and around the globe.

I have witnessed only *a small piece* of this through my work on *How Right Now*, but I want to take what I do know and what I have learned from my time working under the response as well as *all* of the information that I have shared with you in this book, and lay out my thoughts about what our challenges are, what we need to address to do a better job next time, and what we need to get there. I will offer you a vision that is based on my knowledge and my experiences. I will offer you *my* vision for the future of pandemic communication.

Chapter 10

Conclusions, Lessons Learned, and a Vision for the Future

> *Ultimately, the greatest lesson that COVID-19 can teach humanity is that we are all in this together.*
>
> —*Kiran Mazumdar-Shaw*

So, we have come to the end of the book—or almost the end.

Over the course of the last nine chapters, we have discussed a variety of topics related to communicating through a pandemic. I began this book by describing where the idea for it came from and also by telling you a little bit about my experiences over the past several years. I shared with you my pandemic story.

Following that, we reviewed a brief history of pandemic communication in Chapter 2. In this chapter, we talked about the differences between pandemics, epidemics, and outbreaks, and we looked at several examples of pandemics such as the 1918 influenza, HIV/AIDS, Ebola, H1N1, and Zika pandemics. We also looked at the types of communication that were used during each.

In Chapter 3, we took a look at the theoretical underpinnings of pandemic and emergency communication. We discussed the concepts of "emergency response," "crisis communication," and "risk communication" and we reviewed examples from the private sector and examined CDC's CERC framework. We also talked about risk, how people process risk, and the challenges that

DOI: 10.4324/9781003267522-10

emergency and pandemic professionals face in communicating effectively about risk in today's environment.

From there, we explored in Chapter 4 the unique challenges of today's communication environment and how this has impacted our response to COVID. We spent some time talking about the unique aspects of COVID, e.g., its duration, impact, and some of the mitigation strategies employed, and how these have made communicating about the pandemic difficult. Finally, we discussed our current media and communication environment—which is driven in large part by dramatic headlines, entertainment news, and mis- and disinformation—and how that has also complicated matters.

Following this discussion, in Chapter 5, we explored how the pandemic has unfolded over the past several years and the various phases of messaging that we have been exposed to. We looked at messages that were prominent before COVID was declared a pandemic, as well as those that circulated throughout quarantine, reopening, the rollout of the vaccine, and the advent of new variants and boosters.

After this, in Chapter 6, we took a look at how different communities of people have had different experiences in COVID, despite some of the universal aspects of the pandemic. In this chapter, we looked at older adults, teachers, parents, young adults and children, essential workers, healthcare providers, the LGBTQIA community, farm workers/migrant workers, people experiencing homelessness, among others—and we talked a little bit about what each of these groups has gone through.

Then, to go even deeper with you on this topic, we explored in more detail the disproportionate effects the pandemic has had on certain communities in Chapter 7, especially women and racial and ethnic communities. We discussed how the pandemic has brought to light and exacerbated existing racial, social, structural, and economic inequalities. We reviewed the "Social Determinants of Health" framework and began a discussion about how communication can support the conditions that are necessary in order for people to be able to thrive.

To continue this discussion, and build on it, we spent some time in Chapter 8 talking about the numerous communication campaigns and initiatives that have rolled out during the pandemic—and there were many! We started with a review of *How Right Now* that I have had the privilege of leading during the pandemic. Then, we reviewed several other campaigns from the U.S. and around the globe that have focused on a wide variety of topics related to COVID—awareness of the virus, the need to wear masks and socially distance, the roll out of the vaccine, and the mental health impacts. We also discussed the #StopAsianHate movement to better understand the messages and approaches that have been used to raise awareness of and address some of the saddest and most reprehensible aspects of this pandemic.

Then, finally, in Chapter 9, to build on this discussion of *How Right Now*, we spent some time discussing what it was like to lead a team and build a campaign during this time—in a pandemic and in a completely remote work environment. My hope with this chapter was to talk about evidence-based strategies and approaches for building strong teams—especially in difficult circumstances—that may be useful to others doing similar kinds of work. This chapter was based on a mix of my personal experiences and what the literature tells us is important for building good teams. As a result, I offered my interpretation of and thinking about guiding principles and best practices for team building. Things like the importance of communication. The value of setting clear goals and expectations. And how the simple act of saying "thank you" can go a long way with team building—especially in a pandemic.

So, yes, we have covered a lot in this book, but there are a few last pieces that I think are vital to include in order to wrap up this discussion satisfactorily.

I recently read a story[416] in *The New York Times* about how it is inevitable that, over time, many of our memories of this time and this pandemic will fade. The author acknowledged (as a neuroscientist who studies memory and memory disorders like Alzheimer's) how this is not only normal, but in fact, it is necessary for our mental health.

And I see his point. But I also think it is critical that we *not forget* this time entirely. We need to learn from it and we need to remember those learnings so that we can get better at this whole communicating-through-a-pandemic thing. For the next pandemic. And the pandemic after that. And the one after that.

We also need to remember so that we do not forget the issues that have risen in our consciousnesses during this time and so we can really start to address them. Issues like health equity. Racism. Polarization. And mis- and disinformation. If we forget, for the sake of mental health *or whatever*, we will not be any better coming out of this time than we were going into it.

So, as we close out this book, I think it is important to summarize not just what we have discussed over these nine chapters, but also what we have *learned* through it all. What are the main takeaways? What does all of this mean in the context of pandemic communication? And where do we go from here? How do we put all of this to good use in the future?

We will tackle these things over the course of the rest of this chapter.

Lessons Learned

We just reviewed the main topics and tenets that have been covered throughout this book. But what does it all mean? What did we get out of it? Out of all the information I just shared with you in these last couple hundred pages?

What have we learned through this pandemic?

Through it all?
The social distancing?
The quarantine?
The job loss?
The financial hardship?
The sickness and death?
Though the crazy cable news and social media stories?
Have we actually learned anything? I certainly hope so.
I think we have. At least, some things.
Here is what *I* have learned.

Communicating about Health Topics Is Hard

Health is a complex subject. It has to do with how the body works. How the mind works. The interaction of physical systems. It has to do with science.

But it also has to do with how people think about things. What they consider important and whom they trust. It also has to do with their lived experiences and the lens through which they view the world.

And while health, as a topic, may be complex, the specific topics of: "Viruses," "contagions," "transmissibility," "outbreaks," "epidemics," "pandemics," and "vaccinations" are even more complex. These things can vary by *disease*: If, and how, it may be transmitted or contracted; the severity of it and the susceptibility of people to it; and the mitigation and therapeutic strategies that exist to prevent and treat the disease. We saw this in Chapter 2 when we examined different kinds of pandemics. We saw that there were fundamental differences in how the diseases transmitted to and among humans, what the symptoms were, and how transmission could be slowed or prevented.

Further, they can also differ by *person*: Knowledge and understanding of a disease; how people perceive the risks of the disease; whom they trust; how susceptible they believe themselves to be; and the protective factors and measures they have access to and/or are willing to take to protect themselves and that can help guard against negative health outcomes and enable thriving. We discussed this a bit in Chapter 3 when we reviewed risk communication, how people perceive risk, and how they make decisions based on a mix of risk perception and efficacy assessment. We saw through that discussion how people need both—knowledge of the risk as well as the efficacy cues—in order to be able to take the correct steps to protect themselves.

Finally, they can vary by *vaccine*: Whether a vaccine is needed; whether one exists; how it is made; how long it took to create and come to market; its effectiveness. In COVID, reports of people's concerns about the COVID vaccine have been widely shared: It is too new. It came to market too quickly.

Not enough research has been done. We do not know what the long-term side effects are. What is mRNA?

So communicating about health topics is hard. But it gets even harder when one considers that health—and all the topics related to health—also differ by context and experience. As we have seen in Chapters 6 and 7, no one's COVID experience has been exactly the same. Neither are the lenses through which we view and understand health and health-related topics. They are complex and nuanced, which can make communicating about them even harder.

Context Matters

And that means *(yes, you know what I am about to say!)*: Context matters.

I know, we have said this a lot throughout this book. You are probably tired of hearing me say it. But it is true.

Whether you are talking about health more generally, or in COVID, specifically. Where and how we experience health is personal. I do not mean "personal" as in "my health versus your health." It can include that, certainly, but what I really mean by "personal" is that how *I think* about health will be different than how *you think* about it. It could mean that health for me is really just about "my health." But it also could mean that I view my health as being a part of my family's health. Or my community's health. Or my mother's health. Or my child's health.

Health is also situational. It is a product of our lived experiences and related to the lens we have on the world. It is closely tied to our experiences navigating the world and is connected to the settings and structures in which we live, work, play, and worship. It is related to traditions and customs. And to social hierarchies. And to legacies and histories.

Context *has* influenced how we have experienced the pandemic. It has affected the messages we have been exposed to. The information that we have had access to. And, based on this, how we have perceived the pandemic over time. It has enabled and inhibited health and well-being, depending on the structures and settings within which we exist. And as part of this, it has reinforced our sense of financial (in)security. Further shaped our perceptions of health and safety. And intensified our connection to sickness and death. It also has impacted our outlook on the future.

Context has mattered.

Investment in Public Health Infrastructure Is Critical

The challenges we have experienced in COVID, though, have not just had to do with the complexity of these topics, the challenges that come with communicating about them, or people's individual experiences. Rather, the pandemic has made it immensely clear that we are woefully unprepared to handle emergency situations like COVID. In the U.S., but also globally.

This can be seen in the inconsistent ways that countries have handled the pandemic. The mixed messaging. The lack of coordination. The tensions between wealthier and poorer countries for access to vaccines. These have all complicated the global response to COVID.

Yet, a coordinated and consistent global response is *required* to effectively combat global crises like COVID. Because they affect us all. COVID has not cared how rich or poor you are. Or where you live. Or what language you speak. Or what religion you believe. Or what political orientation you have. COVID has not paid attention to the barriers of time and space; rather, the world has been its feeding ground.

Despite this, we have not always been coordinated or consistent. And we are still here—I am writing these pages in *the third year* of the pandemic!—because we have not done a good job of coming together, coordinating, and tackling this problem as a global society. We have acted as islands. Both internationally as well as here in the U.S.

And that has been our downfall.

Now, we can all point fingers and find numerous reasons for why this may be the case, but the fact is that we are where we are, in large part, because we have not prioritized public health in this country or around the world *nearly enough*.

In the U.S., funding for public health has generally been decreasing over the last couple of decades. According to an analysis conducted by Kaiser Health News and the Associated Press in 2020, spending for state public health departments, since 2010, has dropped by 16% per capita. And for local health departments, it has dropped by 18% per capita.[417,418]

Now, you might be thinking,

16% and 18% do not sound like a lot.

But these cuts have resulted in substantial staff reductions. In fact, since 2008, 38,000 state and local public health jobs have been eliminated. Yet, public health staff are needed to do all types of tasks to keep people and communities safe - here and around the world. Things like:[419,420]

- Tracking the sources of disease;
- Administering vaccinations in clinics;
- Conducting home visits to assist parents of new babies;
- Making sure restaurants are clean;
- Ensuring drinking water is safe;
- Developing recommendations for healthy eating;
- Testing water, foods, and specimens for contamination;

- Tracking community health;
- Promoting and improving health by teaching individuals, families, groups, and communities about health and health care issues;
- Creating awareness about health issues;
- Identifying emerging health issues;
- Creating health policies and regulations;
- Designing the systems that deliver health care to people.

Thus an emaciated workforce have been left to do a pretty big job.

As the Kaiser Health News-Associated Press analysis found,

> *State and local government health workers on the ground are sometimes paid so little that they qualify for public aid. They track the coronavirus on paper records shared via fax. Working seven-day weeks for months on end, they fear pay freezes, public backlash and even losing their jobs.*[421,422]

The U.S. Public Health Service (officially known as the Commissioned Corps of the U.S. Public Health Service, or USPHS Commissioned Corps) has traditionally been viewed as one of the world's top public health systems. But without proper support, no system in the world could do the work required to keep the public safe.[423,424]

Declining Trust, Misinformation, Disinformation, and Digital Literacy Are Big Problems

In 2020, the Office of Communications (Ofcom),[425] which is the U.K.'s regulatory agency for the broadcasting, telecommunications, and postal industries, released data that showed that almost half of the adult population in the U.K. have come across mis- or disinformation about COVID. They found, however, that while 55% report that they "[ignore] false claims about coronavirus," up to 40% "are finding it hard to know what is true or false about the virus."[426]

We talked about this in Chapter 4—how our communication environment is messy and convoluted; how the plethora of information that is available to us through multiple channels, in real time, 24-hours-a-day, is overwhelming; how this is enabling the diffusion of false narratives; how it makes it hard to discern what is true, what is false, what is real, and what is fake; and how mis- and disinformation is impacting health decision-making and ultimately, lives.

We also talked in Chapter 4 about how trust is waning—at least here in the U.S.—and how this is contributing to the current crisis of mis- and disinformation.

So, it should not be a mystery to anyone anymore—mis- and disinformation are huge issues. Especially when it comes to public health. And pandemic communication. And to overall trust in science, institutions, and certain types of voices.

This issue of mis- and disinformation—especially given that much of it circulates online and in social media—highlights how important it is for people to be able to discern the information they access through various channels and technologies. This concept, called "digital literacy," is defined by the American Library Association as,

> *The ability to use information and communication technologies to find, evaluate, create, and communicate information, requiring both cognitive and technical skills.*[427]

And the literature tells us that it has an important role to play in helping people navigate the complex communication ecosystem in which we live and make sense of the information they are exposed to.[428–430]

In particular, digital literacy is an important predictor of a person's ability to tell truth from falsehood[431,432] and it becomes incredibly important in times of uncertainty—like the one we have been living in. This is because the research tells us that during times of uncertainty, engaging with information that is trustworthy is *more important than ever.*[433] But when you cannot tell what is true and what is false—and information also keeps changing so you do not know whom to trust and what to believe—it can be hard to know how to make sense of it all.

We Need to Have More Compassion and Understanding for One Another

This time. This pandemic. It has been really hard. And we have all had to deal with really tough things over the course of it.

Sickness.

Death.

Confusion.

Shifting information.

Wrong information.

Loss of jobs.

Loss of freedom.

Loss of control.

All the emotions.

Worry.

Anger.

Fear.

Sadness.

Quarantine.

Mask-wearing.

Social distancing.

Vaccination.

Testing.

Boosting.

Tension in our families.

Disagreements with our friends.

Fights between complete strangers.

Hate, xenophobia, and violence.

Many of us did not really know about or understand very well many of these things just a few years ago. Yet, now, they are a part of our regular vocabulary. Our reality. Our "new normal."

And while, yes, there certainly have been glimmers of hope and joy over the past several years, it has seemed, at times, like we lost our sense of humanity. Our compassion for others. Our recognition that we are all connected and that someone else's well-being impacts our own well-being—especially in a pandemic.

We are a global society, and our lives are intertwined, whether we like it or not. We talked a little bit about this in Chapter 7: How we are all interconnected and how, especially in a pandemic, we all have a role to play in the health of others and their ability to thrive.

We need to understand the plight of others more. We need to have empathy for what others have gone, and are going, through. We need to remember this and sometimes just give people a pass.

This time. This experience. It has all been so hard—on all of us. We have all struggled. And we need to understand that. And acknowledge it.

Despite our differences of opinions.

Despite our differing beliefs.

Despite the fighting.

We need to be cognizant of this.

We need to have compassion.

Let's try not to forget that.

So where do we go from here?

Thus far, I have laid out for you what I have learned during this time and I think there are several implications of these learnings that are worth discussing as we look to the future. Now, I want to take these learnings and propose a vision for the future of pandemic communication.

Developing a Vision for the Future of Pandemic Communication

The COVID pandemic has shown how we, as one global community, can only be safe if everyone is included and protected. And I have to say that I do not think we have done that very well, given what we have experienced over the course of the past several years.

Mis-messaging.

Unclear messaging.

Political fighting.

Politicization of health issues.

Misinformation.

Racism and hate crimes.

Bad actors intentionally spreading lies about the virus and the vaccine.

Indeed, there have been a lot of missteps during this time.

But there have also been a lot of successes in this pandemic. The emergence of a *new vaccine* built on technology that allowed it to come to market faster than *any other vaccine in history*. That is amazing.

It is also a really good vaccine. One of the best available. Which is incredible.

And we have a renewed focus on relationships and a new appreciation for activities that we may have once taken for granted. I know I do.

To learn from this time, though—to *really* learn so that we can get better at this kind of thing when the next pandemic happens *('cuz you know it will!)*—we need to go beyond just documenting what we did wrong and right. We need to take all of this information and turn it into something bigger.

We need a vision for what the future of pandemic communication should look like.

But before I dig into what I think a vision for the future of pandemic communication looks like, I want to reiterate:

I am not an epidemiologist.

I do not pretend to be one.

And while I have had the immense honor of serving in my own small way under the U.S. response to COVID, my experience pales in comparison to the tens of thousands of public health professionals who have given up so much of their lives over the past several years to work on the many, varied dimensions of our pandemic response—in the U.S. and around the world.

What I am is a health communicator, and this is a book focused on pandemic communication. So I offer the following points based on what I have experienced. What I know. What I have observed. And what I have learned from others.

The vision I want to lay out is focused on addressing key challenges that we have faced as a public health community and a global society during this pandemic—but they are mostly communication-focused. As such, there are likely many other dimensions of pandemic response that need to be addressed and improved for the future. I will not address those here.

This is my vision.

Take it. Use it. Add to it. Adapt it.

What matters is that we do not lose the lessons from this time. Let's commit to getting better. Doing better. Being better.

Because we will be here again. Maybe in a month. Maybe a year. Maybe two. Maybe in twenty years. I do not know. In fact, as I write these pages, we are already struggling with a new outbreak of Monkeypox.

So whenever the next pandemic does hit, we need to be prepared, and we should not be starting from scratch. There is no need. We have the foundation. We have been through pandemics before. And we now have lots of lessons learned from *this* pandemic. We can only keep improving.

Articulating My Vision for the Future of Pandemic Communication

The discussions we have had over the last couple hundred pages of this book signal three key dimensions that, I believe, are what we should be striving to achieve in order to do a better job of communicating through the next pandemic. These are:

- Reconceptualizing the idea of "surveillance" to include ongoing non-epidemiological data collection;
- Embracing a more nimble, responsive, inclusive, and collaborative communication "culture";
- Developing strategies and policies that address the mis- and disinformation crisis that currently exists.

We will review each of these below.

Reconceptualizing the idea of "surveillance" to include ongoing non-epidemiological data collection

The first dimension of my vision has to do with broadening our conceptualization of what it means to conduct "surveillance" in relation to pandemic planning and response—for today's modern context.

But first, let's talk about what the word "surveillance" means. The term "surveillance" comes from the French word, "surveiller," which means "to watch over,"[434] and we currently define it as,

> *The ongoing, systematic collection, analysis, and interpretation of health-related data essential to planning, implementation, and evaluation of public health practice.*[435]

The aim of "surveillance" is to:

> *Provide information that can be used for health action by public health personnel, government leaders, and the public to guide public health policy and programs.*[436]

Our current conceptualization of "surveillance," however, has primarily focused on the tracking and collection of data related to disease, illness, and other health events, with use cases for this kind of "surveillance" including:

- The identification of patients and their contacts for treatment and intervention;
- The detection of epidemics, health problems, and changes in health behaviors;
- The estimation of the magnitude and scope of health problems;
- The measurement of trends and characterization of disease;
- The tracking of changes in infectious and environmental agents;
- The assessment of effectiveness of programs and control measures;
- The development of hypotheses and areas of research to address health problems.[437]

As a result, this current conceptualization fundamentally misses the role that culture and lived experience play in understanding how a community perceives, and will react to, the threat of a disease. So, for instance, to understand how a disease may be impacting a community, we need to, of course, track case levels; however, to help guide effective public health policy and programs in response to a disease outbreak, an understanding of the community's lived experiences, knowledge of and beliefs about health topics, and an appreciation of cultural backgrounds, languages, and the lenses through which community members view and navigate the world ought to also be included.

Context matters here too.

Context matters in surveillance.

But we currently *do not* track these perspectives and worldviews systematically or on a regular basis. Therefore, I think we need to broaden our understanding of what we mean by "surveillance" to include not just disease tracking, but also, ongoing and regular audience research and community outreach and engagement.

Just as traditional "surveillance" captures the emergence and spread of contagions, this kind of "social science surveillance" will help capture what and how people are thinking, feeling, and experiencing in terms of pandemic-related topics and information. It also will help understand where people are getting their information and to whom they turn and trust for such information.

This can help keep "a finger on the pulse" of what is going on in communities, across the country, and on a global scale in terms of people's knowledge, attitudes, and beliefs about topics related to outbreaks and pandemics. It also can help ensure the inclusion of diverse perspectives in the development of related policies and programs. It also can help build trust with communities over time – which will help solve many of the other issues we have been talking about in this book. Finally, it can help public health professionals be better prepared to address needs when a pandemic hits.

Embracing a more nimble, responsive, inclusive, and collaborative pandemic communication "culture"

The second dimension of my vision is that we change the "culture" of pandemic communication. This means, first and foremost, that we become more nimble and responsive to the changing directions and needs of a pandemic. I hope that future pandemic communication approaches will embrace the uncertainty—the shifting knowledge—and embody the idea that pandemic messaging is time-bound and, as such, may only be effective in a particular moment. Based on the knowledge *of that moment.*

We have often seen in this pandemic the confusion that has happened with shifts in messaging. And we have discussed this a bit in Chapter 5.

Masks, no masks.

Cloth masks. No, N95 masks.

Variants.

Quarantine.

Vaccines, boosters. One dose, two doses, three doses.

It can be confusing when we try and communicate emerging science and knowledge as "absolute" while things are still changing and evolving, and as we are still learning. As Dr. Saad Omer Director of the Yale Institute for Global Health and Associate Dean at the Yale School of Medicine said,

> *You are seeing sausages being made—in front of the world's eyes.*

We need to get comfortable with the conditional nature of pandemic communication. We need to be OK with saying that we do not know the answer to something and that the recommendations we are messaging about are based on our *current and time-dependent* knowledge.

Changing our communication "culture" also means that we need to re-evaluate the complexity of our communication strategies and approaches. In public health, we are often focused on theory and evidence-based approaches, which are critical to developing sound communication practices and ensuring audience-centered approaches.

Yet, these can sometimes come across as overly complex to public health professionals who are doing this work (maybe for the first time) and who are overworked, underpaid, and overwhelmed—especially during a pandemic. We need to find ways to help the professionals doing this kind of pandemic communication work do it simply, quickly, and effectively. All the while, still applying best practice approaches and principles.

As well, changing the "culture" of pandemic communication means that we are more inclusive of others whose voices are often missed, ignored, silenced, and forgotten. One of the biggest takeaways from this pandemic—and, I hope, this book—is how we have not done right by these voices. Our communication approaches need to start to address the unique contexts of individuals and communities—and in order to do this, we need to have more diverse voices and perspectives at the table helping to make decisions, informing our communication approaches, and ensuring that people from all walks of life are included and supported.

An expansion and reconceptualization of what it means to conduct "surveillance" will help with this, but it also takes intention to be inclusive. To recognize that our country and our world is diverse and multi-faceted. And that a one-size-fits-all approach to communication will not only *not work* in today's world but will also be detrimental to building trust with communities and achieving positive health outcomes now and into the future. We all have a stake in the health of our global society and the only way to effectively improve that health is to make sure that the voices that are often underrepresented are involved and acknowledged.

Finally, changing the "culture" of pandemic communication means that we are more collaborative with each other—both here in the U.S. but also across the globe. It means recognizing the importance of working together and communicating together—no matter where you are in the world. What language you speak. What political affiliation you hold or belief system you follow. Only by working as a global team can we effectively address future pandemics that do not know the boundaries of time and space.

My hope is that if we can change our pandemic communication "culture," our messaging and dissemination strategies will reflect this new culture and enable trust, rather than weaken it. This, in turn, can help address public health issues, for *all* communities—both during future pandemics but also in advance of them.

Developing strategies and policies that address the mis- and disinformation crisis

The final dimension of the vision I want to lay out for you here is that we develop strategies and approaches that can help address the mis- and disinformation and digital literacy problems that currently exist. Those which have made the already difficult job of communicating about pandemics even harder, as we have seen in the context of the COVID pandemic.

Key to this is an attention to and investment in educating people about how to discern what they read, hear, and see. How to know what is factual. And what is not. Who is trustworthy. And who is not. And to do this, we first need to know more about this issue. We need to understand how it works and why it works so well. We need more research into how to identify mis- and disinformation. How to track it. Deal with it. And get out ahead of it. And this means working with researchers, scientists, and other experts in the field who understand what people attend to more and why. What people share more and why. How technology enables this. And how this influences people's information seeking and exposure experiences.

This also requires a proactive approach to working with technology companies to address the rapid, widespread, and unchecked dissemination of inaccurate and blatantly wrong information across digital and social media platforms. Now, yes, technology moves more quickly than policy does, but that should not mean that we do not try to do something now. Working with these companies is vital to being able to figure out how to balance giving people the freedom to talk and share while not supporting the widespread dissemination of information that is false and harmful.

Finally, it means advocating for change at the policy level. This means advocating for protective tools that help people understand what they are hearing, reading, or viewing. Enacting structural changes that enable the vetting of content for accuracy and clarity. Creating cues for people that strengthen their trust in a source rather than weaken it. And developing awareness campaigns, training, and educational programs that improve our digital literacy, help people better navigate what they are exposed to, and bolster trust in scientific information and sources.

Achieving This Vision

I know this is a big vision with lofty goals. And there is a lot of work to do if we want to achieve even just a small part of it.

An expansion of our conceptualization of "surveillance" requires massive shifts in the way we think about disease tracking. It also requires an influx of funding to support ongoing health communication-related research. But there is a vital need to do this, as Dr. Judy Munroe, of the CDC Foundation, said,

> *The needs of a robust public health workforce are diverse and [include] deep knowledge of communities and lived experiences.*[438]

As well, creating a more nimble and responsive pandemic communication strategy that works at the local, national, and global levels is complex with many variables that need to be taken into consideration. The next pandemic may present us with a new and different virus that will likely need new science to understand, treat, and prevent it. This will require a whole new set of tailored messaging that takes into account the policies, laws, regulations, and cultural beliefs and perspectives of the particular community or communities that are affected and for which the messages are intended.

But if we can take all of the knowledge we have from prior pandemics (e.g., how viruses transmit, the mitigation and therapeutic strategies that have worked in the past), and everything we have learned from this one (e.g., rapid vaccine development, how to communicate about pandemics in our current media environment), and develop a more coordinated, nimble, and transparent messaging approach—and we do so more quickly and earlier in the process—we may be able to avoid some of the confusion and resistance that we have seen during this pandemic.

Finally, the ability to address mis- and disinformation and digital literacy is a big task—and maybe it's too late for this. Maybe it's impossible to address it now. The genie *is* already out of the bottle, after all.

But we need to try.

To do this, we need both regulatory and educational approaches that can enable people to better navigate this world. Better understand what they are exposed to. And make better informed decisions so that they may lead healthier and happier lives.

So how do we do it?

Achieving this vision will require a substantial investment of resources in order to be successful. And this "investment" is multi-faceted.

First, it requires more money for public health programs and activities. It means investing in health as part of our national infrastructure and security. Viruses know no borders, after all. They know no boundaries. As Dr. Anan Parekh, the Chief Medical Advisor at the Bipartisan Policy Center, said,

> *I think it's time we communicate to the nation as well as policy makers that if public health isn't part of our nation's infrastructure, I don't what is. It's exactly what everyone takes for granted and yet it's necessary to ensure the conditions that populations can be healthy.*[439]

It also requires more resources to support a broader conceptualization of what surveillance and preparedness really mean. One that includes audience research. Issue identification. And the examination of trusted messages and messengers on an ongoing basis.

It also means investing in people. It means building up the workforce through training and recruitment. We need to train more people for the future of this field. We also need to provide ongoing training so that public health professionals can continue to do their jobs to the best of their abilities.

It means hiring the right amount of and types of staff to support increased levels of activity before, during, and after pandemics. Right now, the field hires surge staff to support increased needs during an emergency—and this will always be a crucial part of responding to crises; however, appropriately staffing the work from the outset—independent of emergency situations—is vital so that the work can be adequately supported in advance of one.

Finally, it means diversifying the workforce and investing in training and recruitment of staff from *all* types of communities, especially those that are most often the hardest hit and that have not been included historically. We discussed in Chapters 6 and 7 how different audiences have had varied experiences throughout the course of the pandemic, and how the pandemic also has impacted different communities unevenly. This signals just how important it is to have representation from a variety of perspectives in the public health field—especially as it relates to health communication. As Dr. J. Nadine Gracia, President and CEO of Trust for America's Health, says,

> *It means we have to focus on leadership and a workforce, ... and ensuring the recruitment and retention of a diverse and inclusive workforce that has the capacities and competencies to address 21ˢᵗ century public health challenges.*[440]

To do this right, context will matter.

Conclusion

So NOW we have come to the end of the book.

At the outset, I told you that I started writing this as a way to process what this time in the pandemic—these last several years—has meant to me, and how I have felt about all of this.

At the beginning of this book, I noted that I thought I was ok, but was not quite sure. But after writing these pages, I do think I can say that writing this book has helped me.

Process.

Understand.

And make sense of it all. Make some sense of this time.

I hope that maybe this book has done something similar for you too. But if not, that is ok. I hope, at least, that maybe you learned something from it.

Because we have covered A LOT.

We have covered numerous topics related to pandemic communication over these last two hundred pages or so: Its history. Our media environment. Different communication and messaging approaches. People's experiences in this pandemic. The disparities that COVID has brought to light. Team building.

We also talked through a vision for the future of pandemic communication that hopefully will enable us to more successfully respond to and address the next pandemic, and the pandemics that come after that. My "vision" areas (redefining "surveillance;" communicating more strategically, nimbly, inclusively, and collaboratively; and addressing mis- and disinformation and digital literacy comprehensively) collectively signal the need to develop and advance a new public health agenda for the 21st century. One that is based in science but also one that engenders trust. To achieve this, we need:

- More trained staff who represent diverse perspectives;
- More transparent and nimble communication;
- More money for programs;
- More ongoing and consistent surveillance that includes community outreach and engagement;
- And more policy and advocacy work that aims to ensure that people are being given accurate and true information with which to make decisions.

This is a big "ask." A big plan. I know.

And it will take all of us to make it a reality.

It has taken a village to get us to where we are today. I say "village" because that is what the public health community is—it is a community of people who are working together toward a common goal, in this case, the common aim of helping improve lives. And they are some of the most dedicated people I have ever known.

But it is also a "village" because that community—with the weight of the world (literally, the world) on their shoulders—is still too small. They cannot do everything that they have on their plates, and do them well, without more help. More support. More people. And more money.

No one could.

We need to do better by them. By all of us. And *for* all of us.

We need to advocate for a better, bigger, stronger, brighter vision of the future of public health. And it will require more than a village to be able to achieve that.

In closing, I want to acknowledge all the public health professionals out there—many of whom are my friends, colleagues, collaborators, clients, and confidants.

These last couple of years have been tough for all of us, but I have been impressed—and continue to be impressed—by your dedication, commitment, strength, and compassion throughout it all.

To all of you, who are working daily to improve health. To save lives. And to make life a little better for people. For the rest of us.

Thank you.

Notes

1. Wardle, C., and Derakhshan, H. Thinking about 'information disorder': Formats of misinformation, disinformation, and mal-information. Journalism, 'Fake News' & Disinformation. UNESCO; 2018:12.
2. Ibid.
3. https://www.nytimes.com/2020/04/09/us/quarantine-mental-health-gender.html
4. http://https://www.nytimes.com/2020/04/09/us/quarantine-mental-health-gender.html
5. https://www.nytimes.com/2021/04/19/well/mind/covid-mental-health-languishing.html
6. https://www.rollingstone.com/culture/culture-features/corona-exhausted-moral-fatigue-974311/
7. https://www.bbc.com/worklife/article/20201203-why-the-pandemic-is-causing-spikes-in-break-ups-and-divorces
8. https://www.pewresearch.org/2021/03/05/in-their-own-words-americans-describe-the-struggles-and-silver-linings-of-the-covid-19-pandemic/
9. https://onlinelibrary.wiley.com/doi/10.1111/acem.14211
10. https://journals.sagepub.com/doi/full/10.1177/1359105321999088
11. https://www.bloomberg.com/news/articles/2021-01-05/divorces-and-marriages-tumbled-in-u-s-during-covid-study-shows
12. https://www.cdc.gov/howrightnow/index.html
13. https://www.cdc.gov/howrightnow/espanol/index.html
14. https://www.cdc.gov/csels/dsepd/ss1978/lesson1/section11.html
15. https://www.npr.org/sections/goatsandsoda/2022/03/11/1085839027/coronavirus-faq-what-does-endemic-mean-and-are-we-there-yet
16. https://www.cdc.gov/csels/dsepd/ss1978/lesson1/section11.html
17. Ibid.
18. Ibid.
19. Ibid.
20. https://www.publichealth.columbia.edu/public-health-now/news/epidemic-endemic-pandemic-what-are-differences
21. https://apic.org/monthly_alerts/outbreaks-epidemics-and-pandemics-what-you-need-to-know/

22. https://www.cdc.gov/csels/dsepd/ss1978/lesson1/section11.html
23. https://www.publichealth.columbia.edu/public-health-now/news/epidemic-endemic-pandemic-what-are-differences
24. Last, J.M., editor. *A dictionary of epidemiology,* 4th edition. New York: Oxford University Press; 2001.
25. https://www.cdc.gov/csels/dsepd/ss1978/lesson1/section11.html
26. https://www.who.int/influenza/resources/documents/pandemic_phase_descriptions_and_actions.pdf
27. https://www.cdc.gov/onehealth/basics/zoonotic-diseases.html
28. Ibid.
29. https://www.who.int/influenza/resources/documents/pandemic_phase_descriptions_and_actions.pdf
30. https://www.healthline.com/health/worst-disease-outbreaks-history
31. https://www.cdc.gov/flu/pandemic-resources/1918-commemoration/1918-pandemic-history.htm
32. https://www.duluthnewstribune.com/community/history/5009517-In-1918-Duluth-faced-pandemic-fire-and-World-War-I
33. https://theconversation.com/weve-known-about-pandemic-health-messaging-since-1918-so-when-it-comes-to-coronavirus-what-has-australia-learnt-134797
34. Ibid.
35. https://www.who.int/data/gho/data/themes/hiv-aids
36. https://www.unaids.org/en/resources/fact-sheet
37. https://www.hiv.gov/hiv-basics/overview/data-and-trends/statistics
38. https://www.kff.org/global-health-policy/fact-sheet/the-global-hivaids-epidemic/
39. https://www.cdc.gov/mmwr/preview/mmwrhtml/mm5521a1.htm
40. https://www.cdc.gov/flu/pandemic-resources/2009-h1n1-pandemic.html
41. https://www.alamy.com/1980s-era-hiv-aids-prevention-public-service-poster-image217297245.html
42. https://www.cdc.gov/flu/pandemic-resources/2009-h1n1-pandemic.html
43. https://www.thebody.com/slideshow/11-sexy-campaigns-that-spread-the-word--and-the-lo
44. Ibid.
45. https://www.cdc.gov/h1n1flu/business/toolkit/additionalcommunicationresources.htm
46. https://www.ncbi.nlm.nih.gov/books/NBK54192/
47. https://www.campaignlive.co.uk/article/doh-ad-campaign-combat-swine-flu-crisis/902135
48. https://www.cdc.gov/vhf/ebola/history/2014-2016-outbreak/index.html
49. Ibid.
50. https://www.who.int/health-topics/middle-east-respiratory-syndrome-coronavirus-mers#tab=tab_1
51. https://www.npr.org/sections/goatsandsoda/2014/08/11/338666715/graphic-warnings-ebola-posters-keep-the-virus-on-pepoles-minds
52. https://www.cdc.gov/zika/transmission/blood-transfusion.html#:~:text=To%20date%2C%20there%20have%20been,have%20been%20documented%20in%20Brazil

53. https://www.usatoday.com/story/money/business/2014/10/24/ebola-in-new-york-media-coverage/17849823/
54. https://www.who.int/emergencies/situations/zika-virus-outbreak
55. https://www.cdc.gov/zika/transmission/blood-transfusion.html#:~:text=To%20date%2C%20there%20have%20been,have%20been%20documented%20in%20Brazil
56. https://www.who.int/news-room/fact-sheets/detail/zika-virus
57. Ibid.
58. https://www.cdc.gov/ncbddd/birthdefects/microcephaly.html#:~:text=Microcephaly%20is%20a%20condition%20where,in%20a%20smaller%20head%20size.
59. https://www.cdc.gov/zika/zap/pdfs/presentations/zap-how-to-communicate-effectively.pdf
60. https://time.com/4434194/zika-florida-outbreak-tourist-deals/
61. https://theconversation.com/four-reasons-why-we-shouldnt-forget-abot-zika-75257
62. https://www.cdc.gov/zika/zap/pdfs/presentations/zap-how-to-communicate-effectively.pdf
63. https://www.tandfonline.com/doi/full/10.1080/10810730.2013.840698
64. ECDC. (2009). Effectiveness of behavioural and psychosocial HIV/STI prevention interventions for MSM in Europe. Technical report. Revised edition. Stockholm, Sweden: Author. Retrieved from http://ecdc.europa.eu/en/publications/Publications/0911_TER_Lit_Review_Effect_HIVSTI_prev_interv_for_MSM.pdf
65. ECDC. (2013a). Annual epidemiological report 2012. Reporting on 2010 surveillance data and 2011 epidemic intelligence data. Stockholm, Sweden: Author. Retrieved from http://ecdc.europa.eu/en/publications/Publications/Annual-Epidemiological-Report-2012.pdf
66. ECDC. (2013b). Review of outbreaks and barriers to MMR vaccination coverage among hard-to-reach populations in Europe. Stockholm, Sweden: Author. Retrieved from http://ecdc.europa.eu/en/publications/Publications/MMR-vaccination-hard-to-reach-population-review-2013.pdf
67. ECDC. (2010). Conducting health communication activities on MMR vaccination. Stockholm, Sweden: Author. Retrieved from http://ecdc.europa.eu/en/publications/Publications/1008_TED_conducting_health_communication_activities_on_MMR_vaccination.pdf
68. ECDC. (2012). Communication on immunisation—Building trust. Stockholm, Sweden: Author. Retrieved from http://ecdc.europa.eu/en/publications/Publications/Forms/ECDC_DispForm.aspx?ID=869
69. Framework Partnership Agreement Grant/2009/007 "Establishing a programme for dissemination of evidence-based health communication activities and innovations on communicable diseases for country support in the EU and EEA/EFTA, 2009–12," with a consortium of universities comprised of the Health Promotion Research Centre at the National University of Ireland Galway, as the lead co-ordinating centre, and the Institute for Social Marketing, University of Stirling, Scotland, and the University of Navarra Clinic, Pamplona, Spain.

70. Doyle, P., Sixsmith, J., Barry, M.M., Mahmood, S., MacDonald, L., O'Sullivan, M., Oroviogoichoechea, C., Cairns, G., Guillen-Grima F., and Núñez-Córdoba, J. (2012). Public health stakeholders' perceived status of health communication activities for the prevention and control of communicable diseases across the EU and EEA/EFTA countries. Stockholm, Sweden: ECDC. Retrieved from http://ecdc. europa.eu/en/publications/Publications/20120620_TER_StatusHealthComm.pdf

71. Infanti, J., Sixsmith, J., Barry, M.M., Núñez-Córdoba, J., Oroviogoicoechea-Ortega, C., & Guillén-Grima, F. (2013). A literature review on effective risk communication for the prevention and control of communicable diseases in Europe. Stockholm, Sweden: ECDC. Retrieved from http://ecdc.europa.eu/en/ publications/Publications/risk-communication-literary-review-jan-2013.pdf

72. Poehlman, J.A., Sidibe, T., Jimenez-Magdaleno, K.V., Vazquez, N., Ray, S.E., Mitchell, E.W., and Squiers, L. (2019). Developing and testing the Deten El Zika Campaign in Puerto Rico. *Journal of Health Communication*, 24(12), 900–911.

73. https://www.nasa.gov/feature/honoring-a-teacher-christa-mcauliffe-s-lost-lessons

74. https://www.livescience.com/biggest-natural-disasters-throughout-history

75. CDC (2019). CERC: Psychology of a Crisis. Retrieved 2/23/22 from https:// emergency.cdc.gov/cerc/ppt/CERC_Psychology_of_a_Crisis.pdf

76. https://www.govtech.com/em/strategic-crisis-management-do-emergency-managers-have-a-role.html

77. Ibid.

78. https://www.epa.gov/risk-communication/learn-about-risk-communication# :~:text=Risk%20communication%20is%20communication%20intended, %2C%20Fischoff%2C%20Bostrom%2C%20Atman.

79. https://www.sciencedirect.com/topics/medicine-and-dentistry/history-of-public-health#:~:text=In%20the%20USA%2C%20the%20first,their%20own%20public %20health%20structures.

80. http://https://www.businessinsider.com/uber-deleteuber-protest-hundreds-of-thousands-quit-app-2019-4#:~:text=The%20%23DeleteUber%20movement %20took%20social,International%20Airport%20in%20New%20York.

81. http://https://www.washingtonpost.com/business/2021/12/22/amazon-web-services-experiences-another-big-outage/

82. http://https://mashable.com/article/united-loses-hundreds-of-millions-in-value-after-man-dragged#:~:text=The%20dragger%20becomes%20the%20dragee.& text=United%20Continental%20stock%20had%20a,became%20a%20major %20news%20story.

83. http://https://www.theatlantic.com/health/archive/2019/12/peloton-christmas-gift-controversy/603148/

84. http://https://selfkey.org/facebooks-data-breaches-a-timeline/

85. http://https://www.thecut.com/2021/09/facebook-very-aware-that-instagram-harms-teen-mental-health.html

86. https://www.washingtonpost.com/outlook/2022/01/03/crises-can-turn-into-positive-savvy-businesses/

87. https://www.prweb.com/releases/the_4_best_crisis_communication_examples_of_ all_time_according_to_digital_silk/prweb17143794.htm

88. https://money.cnn.com/2018/02/23/news/kfc-apology-ad-shortage-chicken/index.html
89. https://emergency.cdc.gov/cerc/
90. https://emergency.cdc.gov/cerc/ppt/CERC_Psychology_of_a_Crisis.pdf
91. https://emergency.cdc.gov/cerc/
92. https://www.epa.gov/risk-communication/learn-about-risk-communication#:~:text=Risk%20communication%20is%20communication%20intended,%2C%20Fischoff%2C%20Bostrom%2C%20Atman.
93. https://emergency.cdc.gov/cerc/
94. Witte, K. (1992). Putting the fear back into fear appeals: The extended parallel process model. *Communications Monographs*, 59(4), 329–349.
95. https://news.un.org/en/story/2020/09/1072022
96. https://www.politico.com/news/2021/04/23/trump-bleach-one-year-484399
97. https://www.fda.gov/consumers/consumer-updates/why-you-should-not-use-ivermectin-treat-or-prevent-covid-19
98. https://news.mit.edu/2018/study-twitter-false-news-travels-faster-true-stories-0308
99. Venette, S. J. (2003). *Risk communication in a Highly Reliability Organization: APHIS PPQ's inclusion of risk in decision making.* Ann Arbor, MI: UMI Proquest Information and Learning.
100. https://www.hhs.gov/sites/default/files/surgeon-general-misinformation-advisory.pdf
101. https://www.americansecurityproject.org/public-diplomacy-and-strategic-communication/disinformation/
102. https://www.rockefellerfoundation.org/blog/misinformation-is-the-biggest-threat-to-ending-this-pandemic/
103. https://www.theatlantic.com/sponsored/genentech-2021/how-communication-and-education-can-help/3704/?preview=1
104. https://www.bbc.com/news/newsbeat-43169625
105. https://www.politico.com/news/2021/04/23/trump-bleach-one-year-484399
106. https://www.cdc.gov/mmwr/volumes/69/wr/mm6916e1.htm
107. https://www.forbes.com/sites/robertglatter/2020/04/25/calls-to-poison-centers-spike--after-the-presidents-comments-about-using-disinfectants-to-treat-coronavirus/?sh=2232b8761157
108. https://www.politico.com/news/2021/04/23/trump-bleach-one-year-484399
109. https://journals.plos.org/plosone/article?id=10.1371/journal.pone.0256358
110. https://www.ucsf.edu/news/2021/03/420081/trumps-chinese-virus-tweet-linked-rise-anti-asian-hashtags-twitter
111. https://www.cnn.com/2021/02/16/us/san-francisco-vicha-ratanapakdee-asian-american-attacks/index.html
112. https://www.pbs.org/articles/violence-against-asian-americans
113. https://www.hrw.org/news/2020/05/12/covid-19-fueling-anti-asian-racism-and-xenophobia-worldwide#
114. https://covid19.who.int/
115. https://www.nytimes.com/2021/02/05/world/asia/china-covid-economy.html
116. https://www.cnbc.com/2022/03/16/what-we-know-about-the-economic-impact-of-chinas-covid-spike.html

117. https://www.preventionweb.net/news/covid-19-and-small-island-nations-what-we-can-learn-new-zealand-and-iceland
118. Ibid.
119. http://https://www.pewresearch.org/politics/2022/06/06/public-trust-in-government-1958-2022/
120. https://www.preventionweb.net/news/covid-19-and-small-island-nations-what-we-can-learn-new-zealand-and-iceland
121. https://www.forbes.com/sites/quora/2019/01/23/how-does-todays-digital-media-environment-influence-the-way-we-behave/?sh=247491583d56
122. https://backlinko.com/social-media-users
123. https://www.medialit.org/reading-room/whatever-happened-news
124. Ibid.
125. Ibid.
126. https://apnews.com/article/1f869794361f917ccd2b8e1cc1c964b8
127. https://www.usg.edu/galileo/skills/unit07/internet07_02.phtml
128. https://datatopics.worldbank.org/world-development-indicators/
129. https://www.pewresearch.org/internet/fact-sheet/internet-broadband/
130. https://online.maryville.edu/blog/what-is-digital-media/
131. https://backlinko.com/social-media-users
132. Burke-Garcia, A. (2017). *Opinion Leaders for Health: Formative Research with Bloggers about Health Information Dissemination* (Doctoral dissertation, George Mason University).
133. Burke-Garcia, A. (2019). *Influencing Health: A Comprehensive Guide to Working with Online Influencers.* Routledge.
134. Ibid.
135. Ibid.
136. https://www.statista.com/statistics/218984/number-of-global-mobile-users-since-2010/
137. https://backlinko.com/social-media-users
138. https://www.uswitch.com/mobiles/guides/history-of-mobile-phones/#:~:text=Mobile%20phones%20were%20invented%20as,the%20emergency%20services%20to%20communicate.
139. https://www.pewresearch.org/internet/fact-sheet/mobile/
140. https://www.statista.com/topics/2539/social-sharing/#topicHeader__wrapper
141. https://www.statista.com/statistics/259477/hours-of-video-uploaded-to-youtube-every-minute/#:~:text=As%20of%20February%202020%2C%20more,for%20online%20video%20has%20grown.
142. https://seedscientific.com/how-much-data-is-created-every-day/
143. https://news.mit.edu/2018/study-twitter-false-news-travels-faster-true-stories-0308
144. https://www.hhs.gov/sites/default/files/surgeon-general-misinformation-advisory.pdf
145. https://www.scientificamerican.com/article/information-overload-helps-fake-news-spread-and-social-media-knows-it/
146. https://www.verywellmind.com/what-is-a-cognitive-bias-2794963

147. Shahi G., Dirkson A., and Majchrzak T. (2021). An exploratory study of COVID-19 misinformation on Twitter. *Online Social Networks* and *Media*, Mar, 22: 100104. doi: 10.1016/j.osnem.2020.100104.
148. Himelein-Wachowiak, M., Giorgi, S., Devoto, A., Rahman, M., Ungar, L., Schwartz, H.A., Epstein, D.H., Leggio, L. and Curtis, B. (2021). Bots and misinformation spread on social media: Implications for COVID-19. *Journal of Medical Internet Research*, 23(5), p.e26933.
149. Shao C., Ciampaglia G.L., Varol O., Yang K., Flammini A., and Menczer F. (2018). The spread of low-credibility content by social bots. *Nature Communications*, Nov 20, 9(1): 4787. doi: 10.1038/s41467-018-06930-7.
150. Bessi A., and Ferrara E. (2016). Social bots distort the 2016 U.S. Presidential election online discussion. First Monday, Nov 03, 21(11): 1. doi: 10.5210/fm.v21i11.7090.
151. Badawy A., Ferrara E., and Lerman K. Analyzing the digital traces of political manipulation: The 2016 Russian interference Twitter campaign. IEEE/ACM International Conference on Advances in Social Networks Analysis and Mining (ASONAM); Aug 28–31, 2018; Barcelona, Spain, 2018. pp. 258–265.
152. Yuan X., Schuchard R.J., and Crooks A.T. (2019). Examining emergent communities and social bots within the polarized online vaccination debate in Twitter. *Social Media + Society*, Sep 04, 5(3): 205630511986546. doi: 10.1177/205630511 9865465.
153. Himelein-Wachowiak, M., Giorgi, S., Devoto, A., Rahman, M., Ungar, L., Schwartz, H.A., Epstein, D.H., Leggio, L. and Curtis, B. (2021). Bots and misinformation spread on social media: Implications for COVID-19. *Journal of Medical Internet Research*, 23(5), p.e26933.
154. https://news.mit.edu/2018/study-twitter-false-news-travels-faster-true-stories-0308
155. http://https://www.pewresearch.org/politics/2022/06/06/public-trust-in-government-1958-2022/
156. https://www.niaid.nih.gov/diseases-conditions/coronaviruses
157. https://www.cdc.gov/coronavirus/mers/about/index.html
158. https://www.goodrx.com/conditions/covid-19/what-does-novel-coronavirus-mean-science-medical-definition#:~:text=The%20word%20%E2%80%9Cnovel%E2%80%9D,previously%20seen%20in%20humans.
159. https://www.lexico.com/definition/scientific_method
160. https://www.verywellmind.com/steps-of-the-scientific-method-2795782
161. https://bgr.com/science/china-pneumonia-sickness-outbreak-virus/
162. https://www.courthousenews.com/chinese-pneumonia-outbreak-stirs-fears-of-sars/
163. https://afludiary.blogspot.com/2019/12/china-hubei-provincial-health-committee.html
164. https://www.axios.com/china-pneumonia-oubtreak-wuhan-e2ef8914-6bd7-46db-814d-1609d590ee07.html
165. https://www.forbes.com/sites/brucelee/2020/01/03/a-mystery-pneumonia-has-afflicted-44-people-in-wuhan-china/?sh=a21db614c6c5

166. https://trumpwhitehouse.archives.gov/articles/15-days-slow-spread/
167. https://www.marketwatch.com/story/the-cdc-says-americans-dont-have-to-wear-facemasks-because-of-coronavirus-2020-01-30
168. https://fortune.com/2020/03/10/coronavirus-politicians-quarantine/
169. https://www.cnet.com/health/how-to-prepare-for-a-coronavirus-quarantine-what-to-stock-up-on/
170. https://www.nytimes.com/2020/03/09/nyregion/coronavirus-ny-quarantines.html
171. https://www.latimes.com/science/story/2020-03-13/coronavirus-when-should-i-self-quarantine
172. https://www.ibtimes.com/coronavirus-trump-weighs-quarantine-new-york-nearby-states-2948619
173. https://www.reuters.com/article/usa-bonds/treasuries-benchmark-yield-lower-after-coronavirus-stay-at-home-extension-idUKL1N2BN13Y
174. https://www.washingtontimes.com/news/2020/apr/1/jerome-adams-us-surgeon-general-fed-guidelines-are/
175. https://www.thestreet.com/investing/zoom-hits-record-high-as-stay-at-home-stock-surge-continues
176. https://www.forbes.com/sites/reneemorad/2020/04/30/why-are-covid-19-related-job-losses-hitting-women-harder-than-men/?sh=79deedc16129
177. https://www.cbsnews.com/live-updates/coronavirus-covid-19-news-2020-04-21/
178. https://abcnews.go.com/Health/11-states-issue-formal-stay-home-orders-amid/story?id=69959039
179. https://www.nytimes.com/2020/03/17/opinion/coronavirus-face-masks.html
180. https://www.cdc.gov/coronavirus/2019-ncov/prevent-getting-sick/types-of-masks.html#:~:text=CDC%20recommends%20that%20specially%20labeled,for%20use%20by%20healthcare%20personnel.
181. https://www.nytimes.com/2020/03/17/opinion/coronavirus-face-masks.html
182. https://www.latimes.com/science/story/2021-07-27/timeline-cdc-mask-guidance-during-covid-19-pandemic
183. https://www.who.int/docs/default-source/coronaviruse/situation-reports/20200402-sitrep-73-covid-19.pdf?sfvrsn=5ae25bc7_2#:~:text=An%20asymptomatic%20laboratory%2Dconfirmed,efforts%20in%20some%20countries.
184. https://www.ncbi.nlm.nih.gov/pmc/articles/PMC2646474/
185. https://www.who.int/docs/default-source/coronaviruse/situation-reports/20200402-sitrep-73-covid-19.pdf?sfvrsn=5ae25bc7_2#:~:text=An%20asymptomatic%20laboratory%2Dconfirmed,efforts%20in%20some%20countries.
186. https://www.nytimes.com/2020/03/17/opinion/coronavirus-face-masks.html
187. https://www.latimes.com/science/story/2021-07-27/timeline-cdc-mask-guidance-during-covid-19-pandemic
188. https://www.cdc.gov/media/releases/2020/p0714-americans-to-wear-masks.html
189. Ibid.
190. https://www.reuters.com/article/us-health-coronavirus-usa-senate/trump-contradicts-cdc-director-on-vaccine-masks-he-was-confused-idUSKBN2672PW

191. https://www.salon.com/2020/04/30/laura-ingraham-falsely-claims-urging-people-to-wear-masks-is-a-plot-to-sow-fear-and-intimidation/
192. https://thehill.com/homenews/state-watch/532152-nh-governor-cancels-inauguration-ceremony-citing-concerns-over-armed
193. https://www.bloomberg.com/opinion/articles/2020-07-18/covid-19-quarantines-are-part-of-america-s-disease-fighting-story
194. https://www.newsweek.com/angry-floridians-threaten-citizens-arrest-official-after-mask-mandate-1513088
195. https://www.forbes.com/sites/madhukarpai/2020/10/30/pandemic-or-not-experts-need-to-be-self-aware-and-humble/?sh=3ed995ce4e0b
196. https://www.washingtonpost.com/politics/paloma/the-trailer/2020/05/28/the-trailer-what-we-ve-learned-from-the-great-mask-war/5ece8f77602ff165d3e42ad7/
197. https://www.advisory.com/en/daily-briefing/2020/04/17/coronavirus
198. https://www.washingtontimes.com/news/2020/apr/30/covid-19-persists-but-its-time-for-a-measured-reop/
199. https://www.forbes.com/sites/kenrapoza/2020/04/27/the-fog-of-covid-19-is-lifting/?sh=7876d598b420
200. https://www.washingtonpost.com/opinions/the-future-belongs-to-the-pandemic-pragmatists/2020/05/15/5f79abc4–96de-11ea-82b4-c8db161ff6e5_story.html
201. https://www.cnbc.com/2020/09/09/op-ed-heres-how-we-can-get-the-economy-back-up-and-running.html
202. https://www.forbes.com/sites/coronavirusfrontlines/2020/05/20/how-the-us-can-responsibly-reopen-the-economy-without-causing-a-second-coronavirus-wave/?sh=720735f360fe
203. https://www.cidrap.umn.edu/news-perspective/2020/09/mixed-messages-hamstring-us-covid-19-response
204. https://www.bloomberg.com/opinion/articles/2020-08-23/america-coronavirus-vaccine-challenge-and-how-to-end-the-pandemic
205. https://abcnews.go.com/Health/us-blacks-latinos-remain-covid-19-vaccine-deliberate/story?id=79830353
206. http://forbes.com/sites/alisonescalante/2021/08/26/most-teenagers-want-the-covid-19-vaccine-even-if-their-parents-disagree/?sh=61304f3e1a57
207. https://www.washingtonpost.com/opinions/2021/07/19/facebook-twitter-covid-misinformation-conundrum/
208. https://abcnews.go.com/US/video/biden-set-enact-vaccine-mandates-white-house-address-79927624
209. https://www.cnbc.com/2021/05/13/cdc-says-fully-vaccinated-people-dont-need-to-wear-face-masks-indoors-or-outdoors-in-most-settings.html
210. https://www.verywellhealth.com/vaccine-sentiment-children-5209131#:~:text=According%20to%20our%20survey%2C%20parents,about%20those%20vaccine%20side%20effects.
211. https://www.ozarksfirst.com/life-health/coronavirus/could-covid-vaccine-cause-heart-inflammation-in-children/
212. https://www.homelandsecuritynewswire.com/dr20211202-covid-is-less-risky-to-children-than-covid-vaccines

213. https://www.nbcnews.com/news/us-news/fauci-warns-omicron-variant-raging-world-rcna9293
214. https://www.webmd.com/lung/news/20220127/deaths-due-to-omicron-higher-than-from-delta
215. https://www.msn.com/en-us/news/us/experts-say-the-now-waning-delta-surge-may-be-the-last-major-covid-19-wave/ar-AAOKGEv
216. https://www.forbes.com/sites/williamhaseltine/2021/07/13/the-delta-dilemma-loosening-covid-19-controls-at-a-time-of-increased-danger/?sh=7c92361a2750
217. https://www.newsweek.com/delta-variant-latest-updates-variant-accounts-83-us-covid-19-cases-cdc-says-1611550
218. https://www.cnn.com/2021/11/29/opinions/fighting-omicron-variant-madad-glanville/index.html
219. https://nypost.com/2021/12/17/redefining-fully-vaccinated-as-three-shots-is-on-the-table/
220. http://https://www.cnbc.com/2021/05/13/cdc-says-fully-vaccinated-people-dont-need-to-wear-face-masks-indoors-or-outdoors-in-most-settings.html
221. http://https://www.cnbc.com/2021/07/27/cdc-to-reverse-indoor-mask-policy-to-recommend-them-for-fully-vaccinated-people-in-covid-hot-spots.html
222. https://www.nytimes.com/2020/04/01/learning/learning-about-coronavirus-and-the-class-divide.html
223. https://www.marketwatch.com/story/the-pandemic-has-more-than-doubled-americans-use-of-food-delivery-apps-but-that-doesnt-mean-the-companies-are-making-money-11606340169
224. Ibid.
225. https://www.marketwatch.com/story/the-pandemic-has-more-than-doubled-americans-use-of-food-delivery-apps-but-that-doesnt-mean-the-companies-are-making-money-11606340169
226. https://www.pewresearch.org/fact-tank/2020/06/16/experiences-with-the-covid-19-outbreak-can-vary-for-americans-of-different-ages/
227. https://fenwayhealth.org/fenway-health-policy-brief-outlines-impact-of-covid-19-on-people-living-with-hiv-and-lgbtqia-people/#:~:text=BOSTON%2C%20March%2025%2C%202020%E2%80%94,at%20elevated%20risk%20for%20infection.
228. https://journals.plos.org/plosone/article?id=10.1371/journal.pone.0252101
229. https://www.pewresearch.org/fact-tank/2020/06/16/experiences-with-the-covid-19-outbreak-can-vary-for-americans-of-different-ages/
230. https://www.mayoclinichealthsystem.org/hometown-health/featured-topic/how-the-covid-19-pandemic-is-affecting-caregiving
231. https://pubmed.ncbi.nlm.nih.gov/33998836/
232. https://journals.sagepub.com/doi/full/10.1177/1066480720969194
233. Ibid.
234. Ibid.
235. Ibid.
236. CDC, 2020; "A Timeline of COVID-19 Developments in 2020," 2020.
237. Anderson, 2020.

238. https://www.westga.edu/~distance/ojdla/winter234/pryor_young_chapman_bates234.html
239. https://ieeexplore.ieee.org/document/9381133
240. https://hechingerreport.org/as-we-talk-about-reopening-schools-are-the-teachers-ok/
241. https://ies.ed.gov/ncee/edlabs/regions/pacific/blogs/blog28_reflecting-on-teacher-wellbeing-during-covid-19-pandemic.asp
242. https://www.ed.gov/coronavirus/supporting-students-during-covid-19-pandemic
243. https://www.ncbi.nlm.nih.gov/pmc/articles/PMC7686789/
244. https://www.businessinsider.com/fighting-mask-mandates-harming-students-mental-health-school-covid-psychiatrists-2021-9
245. https://www.youtube.com/watch?v=3oM1spvo3_g&feature=emb_title
246. https://www.epi.org/publication/the-consequences-of-the-covid-19-pandemic-for-education-performance-and-equity-in-the-united-states-what-can-we-learn-from-pre-pandemic-research-to-inform-relief-recovery-and-rebuilding/
247. https://www.washingtonpost.com/education/2020/09/15/america-put-up-or-shut-up-1-trillion-investment-help-kids-poverty/
248. https://www.epi.org/blog/what-teaching-is-like-during-the-pandemic-and-a-reminder-that-listening-to-teachers-is-critical-to-solving-the-challenges-the-coronavirus-has-brought-to-public-education/
249. https://www.epi.org/blog/what-teaching-is-like-during-the-pandemic-and-a-reminder-that-listening-to-teachers-is-critical-to-solving-the-challenges-the-coronavirus-has-brought-to-public-education/
250. https://www.ncsl.org/research/labor-and-employment/covid-19-essential-workers-in-the-states.aspx
251. https://www.brookings.edu/research/to-protect-frontline-workers-during-and-after-covid-19-we-must-define-who-they-are/#:~:text=We%20define%20%E2%80%9Cfrontline%20workers%E2%80%9D%20as,health%20risks%20in%20their%20workplaces.
252. https://www.statista.com/statistics/1221781/us-number-frontline-workers-industry/#:~:text=In%20the%20United%20States%2C%20there,in%20the%20health%20care%20industry.
253. https://www.epi.org/blog/who-are-essential-workers-a-comprehensive-look-at-their-wages-demographics-and-unionization-rates/
254. Ibid.
255. https://www.safetyandhealthmagazine.com/articles/20818-more-than-60-of-essential-workers-and-their-families-may-be-at-higher-risk-of-severe-covid-19-study
256. https://jamanetwork.com/journals/jamainternalmedicine/article-abstract/2772328
257. https://www.safetyandhealthmagazine.com/articles/20818-more-than-60-of-essential-workers-and-their-families-may-be-at-higher-risk-of-severe-covid-19-study
258. https://www.nber.org/digest-202103/measuring-virus-risk-essential-workers-and-dependents
259. https://www.cdc.gov/mmwr/volumes/70/wr/mm7005a3.htm

260. https://www.pewresearch.org/hispanic/2018/11/27/u-s-unauthorized-immigrant-total-dips-to-lowest-level-in-a-decade/
261. https://khn.org/news/article/anti-immigrant-vitriol-complicates-vaccine-rollout-in-southern-states/
262. https://www.farmworkerjustice.org/about-farmworker-justice/who-we-serve/#:~:text=Who%20are%20farmworkers%3F,status%20under%20current%20U.S.%20laws.
263. Duncan, W. (2015). Transnational disorders: Returned migrants at Oaxaca's Psychiatric Hospital. *Medical Anthropology*, 29(1), 24–41. doi:10.1111/maq.12138. PMID 25294096.
264. https://www.bls.gov/charts/census-of-fatal-occupational-injuries/number-and-rate-of-fatal-work-injuries-by-industry.htm
265. https://www.ncbi.nlm.nih.gov/pmc/articles/PMC8081247/
266. https://www.thelancet.com/journals/lanres/article/PIIS2213-2600(21)00068-0/fulltext
267. https://www.ncbi.nlm.nih.gov/pmc/articles/PMC7514392/#:~:text=The%20authors%20found%20that%2028,to%20less%20distress%20among%20HCWs.
268. https://www.kff.org/racial-equity-and-health-policy/issue-brief/covid-19-risks-impacts-health-care-workers-race-ethnicity/
269. https://mhanational.org/mental-health-healthcare-workers-covid-19
270. Santarone, K., McKenney, M., and Elkbuli, A. (2020). Preserving mental health and resilience in frontline healthcare workers during COVID-19. *American Journal of Emergency Medicine*, 38(7), 1530–1531.
271. https://mhanational.org/mental-health-healthcare-workers-covid-19
272. Penwell-Waines, L., Ward, W., Kirkpatrick, H., et al. (2018). Perspectives on healthcare provider well-being: Looking back, moving forward. *Journal of Clinical Psychology in Medical Settings*, 25(3), 295–304.
273. https://www.unhcr.org/en-us/figures-at-a-glance.html
274. https://www.opensocietyfoundations.org/explainers/covid-19-and-undocumented-workers
275. https://time.com/5944806/undocumented-immigrants-covid-19/
276. https://www.unhcr.org/en-us/about-us.html
277. https://reporting.unhcr.org/sites/default/files/COVID-19%20progress%20report%20-%2004.10.20%20-%20FINAL.pdf#_ga=2.216646738.556799215.1628872118-1402846191.1628872118
278. https://endhomelessness.org/homelessness-in-america/homelessness-statistics/state-of-homelessness-report-legacy/#:~:text=There%20are%20an%20estimated%20553%2C742,people%20in%20the%20general%20population
279. https://nhchc.org/covid-dashboard/
280. https://www.cdc.gov/coronavirus/2019-ncov/need-extra-precautions/homelessness.html
281. https://unitedwaynca.org/stories/effect-pandemic-homeless-us/
282. https://www.vera.org/covid-19-if-prison-walls-could-talk
283. https://www.themarshallproject.org/2021/04/23/how-we-survived-covid-19-in-prison

284. https://pubmed.ncbi.nlm.nih.gov/33760428/
285. https://www.chapinhall.org/research/untold-stories-covid-19/
286. https://www.pewresearch.org/fact-tank/2020/06/16/experiences-with-the-covid-19-outbreak-can-vary-for-americans-of-different-ages/
287. https://greatergood.berkeley.edu/article/item/why_is_the_pandemic_so_hard_on_young_people
288. https://udayton.edu/news/articles/2020/12/messinger_covid.php
289. https://www.cdc.gov/vaccines/acip/meetings/downloads/slides-2021-11-2-3/03-COVID-Jefferson-508.pdf
290. https://udayton.edu/news/articles/2020/12/messinger_covid.php
291. Ibid.
292. https://www.pewresearch.org/fact-tank/2020/06/16/experiences-with-the-covid-19-outbreak-can-vary-for-americans-of-different-ages/
293. https://www.chapinhall.org/research/untold-stories-covid-19/
294. Ibid.
295. https://greatergood.berkeley.edu/article/item/why_is_the_pandemic_so_hard_on_young_people
296. https://www.usnews.com/news/health-news/articles/2021-10-08/study-confirms-rise-in-child-abuse-during-covid-pandemic#:~:text=suspected%20child%20abuse.-,Among%20children%20aged%205%20and%20older%2C%20the%20number%20of%20child,went%20into%20effect%20last%20year.
297. https://www.cdc.gov/mmwr/volumes/69/wr/mm6949a1.htm
298. https://fenwayhealth.org/fenway-health-policy-brief-outlines-impact-of-covid-19-on-people-living-with-hiv-and-lgbtqia-people/#:~:text=BOSTON%2C%20March%2025%2C%202020%E2%80%94,at%20elevated%20risk%20for%20infection.
299. https://www.kff.org/coronavirus-covid-19/poll-finding/the-impact-of-the-covid-19-pandemic-on-lgbt-people/
300. https://www.kff.org/coronavirus-covid-19/issue-brief/the-implications-of-covid-19-for-mental-health-and-substance-use/
301. Ibid.
302. https://time.com/6046301/find-community-pandemic/
303. Burke-Garcia, A., Berktold, J., Bailey, L., Wagstaff, L., Thomas, C., Crick, C., Walsh, M., Mitchell, E. W., Vallery Verlenden, J. M., Puddy, R., Mercado, M. C., Xia, K., Aina, T., Caicedo, L., and Nelson, P. (2022). Findings from an assessment of mental health and coping disparities amongst racial and ethnic groups amid COVID-19 from the *How Right Now* Campaign. Manuscript submitted for publication.
304. Burke-Garcia, A., Berktold, J., Rabinowitz, L., Wagstaff, L., W. Thomas, C., Crick, C., Walsh, M. S., Mitchell, E. W., Verlenden, J. M. V., Puddy, R., Xia, K., Aina, T., Caicedo, L., Mercado, M. C. and Nelson, BA, P. (2022). Assessment of Mental Health and Coping Disparities Among Racial and Ethnic Groups Amid COVID-19 From the *"How Right Now"* Campaign. Public Health Reports, 00333549221121667.
305. https://www.brookings.edu/blog/how-we-rise/2021/04/02/indigenous-communities-demonstrate-innovation-and-strength-despite-unequal-losses-during-covid-19/

306. https://www.worldbank.org/en/news/feature/2020/05/19/community-responses-to-covid-19-from-the-horn-of-africa-to-the-solomon-islands
307. https://www.aarp.org/work/job-search/coronavirus-occupation-job-loss/
308. https://www.hcinnovationgroup.com/population-health-management/social-determinants-of-health/article/21133730/for-vulnerable-populations-covid-is-a-fun-house-mirror-amplifying-issues-that-have-existed-forever
309. https://www.cdc.gov/howrightnow/index.html
310. Personal conversation, February 24, 2022.
311. https://child-foundation.org/what-is-child/child-disorders/neuroendocrine-hyperplasia-of-infancy-nehi/
312. https://www.nia.nih.gov/health/what-are-palliative-care-and-hospice-care
313. https://www.statista.com/topics/5994/the-coronavirus-disease-covid-19-outbreak/#dossierKeyfigures
314. Ibid.
315. https://www.kff.org/global-health-policy/issue-brief/economic-impact-of-covid-19-on-pepfar-countries/#:~:text=The%20toll%20the%20COVID%2D19,downturn%20since%20the%20Great%20Depression.
316. https://www.statista.com/topics/6139/covid-19-impact-on-the-global-economy/#dossierKeyfigures
317. https://www.kff.org/global-health-policy/issue-brief/economic-impact-of-covid-19-on-pepfar-countries/#:~:text=The%20toll%20the%20COVID%2D19,downturn%20since%20the%20Great%20Depression.
318. https://www.cdc.gov/mmwr/volumes/70/wr/mm7015e2.htm
319. https://www.pnas.org/doi/full/10.1073/pnas.2014746118
320. https://journals.sagepub.com/doi/10.1177/00333549211026799
321. https://medicine.yale.edu/news-article/health-notes-people-of-color-suffer-disproportionate-impact-of-covid-19-pandemic/
322. https://www.cdc.gov/mmwr/volumes/70/wr/mm7005a3.htm
323. Kearney, A., Hamel, L., and Brodie, M. Mental health impact of the covid-19 pandemic: An update. Kaiser Family Foundation (KFF). https://www.kff.org/coronavirus-covid-19/poll-finding/mental-health-impact-of-the-covid-19-pandemic/. Published April 14, 2021.
324. Anderson, K.N., Radhakrishnan, L., Lane, R.I., Sheppard, M., DeVies, J., Azondekon, R., Smith, A.R., Bitsko, R.H., Hartnett, K.P., Lopes-Cardozo, B. and Leeb, R.T. (2022). Changes and inequities in adult mental health-related emergency department visits during the COVID-19 pandemic in the US. *JAMA Psychiatry*.
325. http://https://www.mayoclinic.org/diseases-conditions/coronavirus/expert-answers/coronavirus-infection-by-race/faq-20488802
326. Burke-Garcia, A., Berktold, J., Bailey, L., Wagstaff, L., Thomas, C., Crick, C., Walsh, M., Mitchell, E. W., Vallery Verlenden, J. M., Puddy, R., Mercado, M. C., Xia, K., Aina, T., Caicedo, L., and Nelson, P. (2022). Findings from an assessment of mental health and coping disparities amongst racial and ethnic groups amid COVID-19 from the *How Right Now* Campaign. Manuscript submitted for publication.
327. https://jamanetwork.com/journals/jamapsychiatry/fullarticle/2790337

328. https://www.npr.org/sections/goatsandsoda/2021/03/26/980480882/why-pandemics-give-birth-to-hate-from-black-death-to-covid-19

329. McKnight-Eily, L.R., Okoro, C.A., Strine, T.W., et al. (2021). Racial and ethnic disparities in the prevalence of stress and WORRY, mental health conditions, and INCREASED substance use among adults during the Covid-19 Pandemic—United States, April and May 2020. MMWR Morbidity and Mortality Weekly Report, 70(5), 162–166. doi:10.15585/mmwr.mm7005a3

330. https://www.chapinhall.org/research/untold-stories-covid-19/

331. https://wmpllc.org/ojs/index.php/jem/article/view/2958

332. https://www.pewresearch.org/fact-tank/2016/07/01/racial-gender-wage-gaps-persist-in-u-s-despite-some-progress/

333. https://jamanetwork.com/journals/jamainternalmedicine/article-abstract/2772328

334. Newkirk, V.R. II (June 17, 2016). A Generation of Bad Blood. *The Atlantic*. Archived from the original on December 18, 2020. Retrieved December 18, 2020.

335. Baker, S.M., Brawley, O.W., and Marks, L.S. (June 2005). Effects of untreated syphilis in the negro male, 1932 to 1972: A closure comes to the Tuskegee study, 2004 (PDF). *Urology*, 65(6), 1259–1262. doi:10.1016/j.urology.2004.10.023. PMID 15922414. Archived (PDF) from the original on September 15, 2012. Retrieved December 18, 2020. The study was officially titled "The Effects of Untreated Syphilis in the Negro Male."

336. "The Tuskegee Timeline". U.S. Public Health Service Syphilis Study at Tuskegee. U.S. Centers for Disease Control and Prevention. Archived from the original on May 10, 2019. Retrieved December 18, 2020. It was called the "Tuskegee Study of Untreated Syphilis in the Negro Male."

337. https://www.cdc.gov/tuskegee/timeline.htm#:~:text=It%20was%20originally %20called%20the,informed%20consent%20was%20not%20collected.

338. Brandt, A.M. (December 1978). Racism and Research: The Case of the Tuskegee Syphilis Study. The Hastings Center Report. Garrison, New York: Wiley-Blackwell, 8(6), 21–29. doi:10.2307/3561468. JSTOR 3561468. PMID 721302. Archived from the original on January 18, 2021. Retrieved June 27, 2020.

339. "Tuskegee Study - Timeline". CDC - NCHHSTP. March 2, 2020. Archived from the original on May 10, 2019. Retrieved May 14, 2020.

340. https://www.theatlantic.com/sponsored/genentech-2021/how-communication-and-education-can-help/3704/

341. https://www.unwomen.org/en/news/stories/2020/9/ feature-covid-19-economic-impacts-on-women

342. https://jamanetwork.com/journals/jama/fullarticle/2771762

343. Coley, R., and Baum, C. (2021). Trends in mental health symptoms, service use, and unmet need for services among us adults through the first nine months of the Covid-19 pandemic. *Translational Behavioral Medicine*, April. doi:10.21203/rs.3 .rs-146306/v1

344. Rothman, S., Gunturu, S., and Korenis, P. (2020). The mental health impact of the COVID-19 epidemic on immigrants and racial and ethnic minorities. *QJM: An International Journal of Medicine*, 113(11), 779–782. doi:10.1093/qjmed/ hcaa203

345. Saltzman, L.Y., Lesen, A.E., Henry, V., Hansel, T.C., and Bordnick, P.S. (2021). Covid-19 mental health disparities. *Health Security*, 19(S1). doi:10.1089/hs.2021.0017

346. https://medicine.yale.edu/news-article/health-notes-people-of-color-suffer-disproportionate-impact-of-covid-19-pandemic/

347. https://journals.sagepub.com/doi/10.1177/0890117119896122d?icid=int.sj-full-text.similar-articles.1

348. https://www.wmpllc.org/ojs/index.php/jem/article/view/2958

349. CDC. (2020). Social determinants of health. https://www.cdc.gov/socialdeterminants/faqs/index.htm#faq10n

350. https://www.who.int/health-topics/social-determinants-of-health

351. https://www.healthypeople.gov/2020/topics-objectives/topic/social-determinants-of-health

352. Burke-Garcia, A., Johnson-Turbes, A., Mitchell, E.W., Verlenden, J.M.V., Puddy, R., Mercado, M.C., Nelson, N., Thomas, T., Crick, C., Leeb, R., Rabinowitz, L., McCutchan, L., Xia, K., Wagstaff, L., Feng, M., Caicedo, L., & Tolbert, E. (2021). *How Right Now:* The role of social determinants of health as they relate to emotional well-being amidst the COVID-19 pandemic. *Journal of Emergency Management*, 19(9), 17–62.

353. https://health.gov/healthypeople/objectives-and-data/social-determinants-health

354. Burke-Garcia, A., Johnson-Turbes, A., Mitchell, E.W., Verlenden, J.M.V., Puddy, R., Mercado, M.C., Nelson, N., Thomas, T., Crick, C., Leeb, R., Rabinowitz, L., McCutchan, L., Xia, K., Wagstaff, L., Feng, M., Caicedo, L., & Tolbert, E. (2021). *How Right Now:* The role of social determinants of health as they relate to emotional well-being amidst the COVID-19 pandemic. *Journal of Emergency Management*, 19(9), 17–62.

355. Fosse, E., Helgesen, M.K., Hagen, S., and Torp, S. (2018). Addressing the social determinants of health at the local level: Opportunities and challenges. *Scandinavian Journal of Public Health*, 46(20_suppl), 47–52.

356. Puig-Barrachina, V., Malmusi, D., Martínez, J. M., and Benach, J. (2011). Monitoring social determinants of health inequalities: The impact of unemployment among vulnerable groups. *International Journal of Health Services*, 41(3), 459–482.

357. Ahnquist, J., Wamala, S.P., and Lindstrom, M. (2012). Social determinants of health – A question of social or economic capital? Interaction effects of socio-economic factors on health outcomes. *Social Science & Medicine*, 74(6), 930–939.

358. Seng, J.S., Lopez, W.D., Sperlich, M., Hamama, L., and Meldrum, C.D.R. (2012). Marginalized identities, discrimination burden, and mental health: Empirical exploration of an interpersonal-level approach to modeling inter-sectionality. *Social Science & Medicine*, 75(12), 2437–2445.

359. Hyman, I. (2009). Racism as a determinant of immigrant health. Ottawa: Strategic Initiatives and Innovations Directorate of the Public Health Agency of Canada.

360. https://wmpllc.org/ojs/index.php/jem/article/view/2958

361. Ibid.

362. Burke-Garcia, A., Berktold, J., Rabinowitz, L., Wagstaff, L., Thomas, C., Crick, C., Walsh, M., Mitchell, E.W., Vallery Verlenden, J.M., Puddy, R., Mercado, M.C., Xia, K., Aina, T., Caicedo, L., Nelson, P., and Johnson-Turbes, A. (2022). Findings from an assessment of mental health and coping disparities amongst racial

and ethnic groups amid COVID-19 from the *How Right Now* Campaign. Manuscript submitted for publication.

363. Anderson, K.N., Radhakrishnan, L., Lane, R.I., Sheppard, M., DeVies, J., Azondekon, R., Smith, A.R., Bitsko, R. H., Hartnett, K.P., Lopes-Cardozo, B. and Leeb, R.T. (2022). Changes and inequities in adult mental health-related emergency department visits during the COVID-19 pandemic in the US. *JAMA Psychiatry*.

364. https://www.cdc.gov/howrightnow/index.html

365. https://www.linkedin.com/learning/social-media-video-for-business-and-marketing

366. https://vimeo.com/440757588?ref=em-share

367. Ettman, C.K., Abdalla, S.M., Cohen, G.H., Sampson, L., Vivier, P.M., and Galea, S. Prevalence of depression symptoms in U.S. adults before and during the covid-19 pandemic. *JAMA Network Open*, 3(9). doi:10.1001/jamanetworkopen.2020.19686

368. Coley, R., and Baum, C. (2021). Trends in mental health symptoms, service use, and unmet need for services among us adults through the first nine months of the Covid-19 pandemic. *Translational Behavioral Medicine*, April. doi:10.21203/rs.3.rs-146306/v1

369. https://www.mhanational.org/research-reports/2021-state-mental-health-america

370. https://www.cdc.gov/howrightnow/

371. https://www.facebook.com/KrisJenner/posts/4585575408150452

372. https://www.facebook.com/MelissaJoanHart/posts/10157382418471541

373. https://www.cdc.gov/howrightnow/

374. Garcia-Burke, A., Rabinowitz Bailey, L., Berktold, J., Wagstaff, L., Thomas, C. W., Crick, C., Mitchell, E. W., Verlenden, J. M. V., Puddy, R. W., Mercado, M. C., Friedman, A., Bruss, K., Xia, K., Sawyer, J., Feng, M., Johnson-Turbes, A., Kappel, R., Afanaseva, D., Nelson, P. (2022). *How Right Now/Que Hacer Ahora:* Findings from an Evaluation of a National Mental Health and Coping Campaign Amidst the COVID-19 Pandemic. [Manuscript submitted for publication].

375. https://www.norc.org/PDFs/How%20Right%20Now/HRN-QHA%20Evaluation%20Special%20Report%20210930.pdf

376. https://www.thedrum.com/creative-works/project/the-ad-council-viacomcbs-alone-together

377. https://www.adweek.com/convergent-tv/viacom-and-ad-council-debut-alonetogether-a-social-campaign-about-social-distancing/

378. https://www.thedrum.com/news/2020/04/08/the-ad-council-and-google-push-stayhome-save-lives-industry-wide-movement

379. https://www.adcouncil.org/learn-with-us/press-releases/mtv-and-viacomcbs-entertainment-youth-group-launch-backtoschooltogether-campaign-in-partnership-with-the-ad-council

380. https://www.theguardian.com/world/2021/feb/24/covid-ad-campaign-launches-to-urge-england-to-stay-at-home

381. https://www.who.int/campaigns/connecting-the-world-to-combat-coronavirus/safehands-challenge

382. https://wfanet.org/knowledge/item/2020/04/08/Stay-Home-Save-Lives

383. https://nursing.duke.edu/news/who-safe-hands-challenge

384. https://www.adcouncil.org/press-releases/the-ad-council-and-covid-collaborative-reveal-its-up-to-you-campaigns-to-educate-millions-of-americans-about-covid-19-vaccines

385. https://www.covidcollaborative.us/

386. https://www.vox.com/22309620/chile-covid-19-vaccination-campaign

387. https://www.usatoday.com/story/news/health/2021/02/25/covid-19-ad-council-vaccine-education-campaign-coronavirus/6808426002/

388. https://www.bloomberg.com/news/newsletters/2021-12-29/the-factors-in-chile-s-covid-success

389. https://www.americasquarterly.org/article/inside-chiles-world-class-vaccination-campaign/

390. https://twitter.com/roddbert/status/1367188095616094213

391. https://www.cdc.gov/coronavirus/2019-ncov/communication/mask-up-america.html

392. https://www.stopasianhate.info/

393. https://www.harpersbazaar.com/culture/politics/a35549052/stop-asian-hate-campaign/

394. https://www.fbi.gov/investigate/civil-rights/hate-crimes

395. https://www.ny1.com/nyc/all-boroughs/news/2022/02/14/hate-crime-increase-2021-asian-american-

396. https://www.cnn.com/2021/02/16/us/san-francisco-vicha-ratanapakdee-asian-american-attacks/index.html

397. https://www.voanews.com/a/anti-asian-crimes-persist-a-year-after-atlanta-spa-shooting/6508964.html

398. https://www.cdc.gov/howrightnow/index.html

399. https://www.cdc.gov/flu/resource-center/toolkit/index.htm

400. https://www.izsummitpartners.org/content/uploads/2014/05/19a-3_Garcia_CDC-National-Influenza-Vaccination-Communications-Campaign.pdf

401. https://www.google.com/url?sa=i&url=https%3A%2F%2Fwww.who.int%2Fin-fluenza_vaccines_plan%2Fresources%2Fsheedy.pdf&psig=AOvVaw0Nt8dq7yVPEg6hJ_SD7S_y&ust=1648227546926000&source=images&cd=vfe&ved=0CAwQjhxqFwoTCMCo35-c3_YCFQAAAAAdAAAAABAO

402. https://www.cdc.gov/flu/resource-center/toolkit/index.htm

403. Ibid.

404. https://www.nytimes.com/guides/business/manage-a-successful-team

405. https://www.masterclass.com/articles/how-to-build-a-strong-team?__cf_chl_capt-cha_tk__=F_y6Ib2Vrpj9aUNAkc0PhdyiqSvhy17uEGWws4brYR0-1641336177-0-gaNycGzNBz0

406. https://medium.com/walmartglobaltech/5-principles-guaranteed-to-help-build-a-strong-team-culture-6055ab478c56

407. https://www.michaelpage.ae/advice/management-advice/development-and-retention/building-effective-team

408. https://medium.com/walmartglobaltech/5-principles-guaranteed-to-help-build-a-strong-team-culture-6055ab478c56

409. https://www.michaelpage.ae/advice/management-advice/development-and-retention/building-effective-team
410. https://medium.com/walmartglobaltech/5-principles-guaranteed-to-help-build-a-strong-team-culture-6055ab478c56
411. https://www.michaelpage.ae/advice/management-advice/development-and-retention/building-effective-team
412. https://medium.com/walmartglobaltech/5-principles-guaranteed-to-help-build-a-strong-team-culture-6055ab478c56
413. https://www.michaelpage.ae/advice/management-advice/development-and-retention/building-effective-team
414. https://medium.com/walmartglobaltech/5-principles-guaranteed-to-help-build-a-strong-team-culture-6055ab478c56
415. https://www.michaelpage.ae/advice/management-advice/development-and-retention/building-effective-team
416. https://www.nytimes.com/2022/03/09/opinion/pandemic-memory.html
417. https://apnews.com/article/e28724a125a127f650a9b6f48f7bb938
418. https://khn.org/news/us-public-health-system-underfunded-under-threat-faces-more-cuts-amid-covid-pandemic/
419. https://zm.tauedu.org/functions-of-public-health/
420. https://www.health.ny.gov/prevention/public_health_works/who_are_public_health_employees.htm
421. https://apnews.com/article/e28724a125a127f650a9b6f48f7bb938
422. https://khn.org/news/us-public-health-system-underfunded-under-threat-faces-more-cuts-amid-covid-pandemic/
423. https://apnews.com/article/e28724a125a127f650a9b6f48f7bb938
424. https://khn.org/news/us-public-health-system-underfunded-under-threat-faces-more-cuts-amid-covid-pandemic/
425. https://www.ofcom.org.uk/about-ofcom/what-is-ofcom
426. https://www.ofcom.org.uk/about-ofcom/latest/features-and-news/half-of-uk-adults-exposed-to-false-claims-about-coronavirus
427. https://literacy.ala.org/digital-literacy/
428. https://misinforeview.hks.harvard.edu/article/digital-literacy-is-associated-with-more-discerning-accuracy-judgments-but-not-sharing-intentions/
429. https://blogs.lse.ac.uk/medialse/2020/06/17/fake-news-covid-19-and-digital-literacy-do-what-the-experts-do/
430. https://shareverified.com/2021/11/10/digital-literacy-is-our-best-weapon-against-misinformation/
431. https://blogs.lse.ac.uk/medialse/2020/06/17/fake-news-covid-19-and-digital-literacy-do-what-the-experts-do/
432. https://www.frontiersin.org/articles/10.3389/fcomm.2021.697383/full
433. https://blogs.lse.ac.uk/medialse/2020/06/17/fake-news-covid-19-and-digital-literacy-do-what-the-experts-do/
434. Centers for Disease Control and Prevention (CDC). Introduction to Public Health. In: *Public Health 101 Series*. Atlanta, GA: U.S. Department of Health and Human Services, CDC; 2014. Available at: https://www.cdc.gov/training/publichealth101/surveillance.html.

435. https://www.cdc.gov/training/publichealth101/surveillance.html#:~:text=Public%20health%20surveillance%20is%20%E2%80%9Cthe,health%20practice.%E2%80%9D%20%E2%80%94%20Field%20Epidemiology

436. Centers for Disease Control and Prevention (CDC). Introduction to Public Health. In: *Public Health 101 Series*. Atlanta, GA: U.S. Department of Health and Human Services, CDC; 2014. Available at: https://www.cdc.gov/training/publichealth101/surveillance.html.

437. Ibid.

438. https://www.linkedin.com/posts/cdc-foundation_light-camera-action-summit-1-report-activity-6897627642472804352-RsWx/

439. Ibid.

440. Ibid.

Index

Note: *Italicized*, **bold** and ***bold italicized*** page numbers refer to figures, tables and boxes. Page numbers followed by "n" refer to notes.

Printed in the United States
by Baker & Taylor Publisher Services